Genetically Modified Organisms, Grade 7

What if you could challenge your seventh graders to become informed citizens by analyzing real-world implications of GMOs? With this volume in the *STEM Road Map Curriculum Series*, you can!

Genetically Modified Organisms outlines a journey that will steer your students toward authentic problem solving while grounding them in integrated STEM disciplines. Like the other volumes in the series, this book is designed to meet the growing need to infuse real-world learning into K–12 classrooms.

This interdisciplinary, five-lesson module uses project- and problem-based learning to help students investigate the opportunities and challenges of GMO production and consumption. Working in teams, students will create a documentary communicating the health, social, and economic aspects of GMO production and consumption. To support this goal, students will do the following:

- Use the Internet and other sources to build knowledge of an issue, and recognize and value stakeholders and their viewpoints in an issue.

- Explore the relationship among local, state, and federal legislation related to GMOs.

- Understand the role of cost-benefit analysis in making informed economic decisions.

- Develop skills to evaluate arguments, create and communicate individual understanding and perspectives.

- Gain a deeper understanding that structure and function are related by examining plants and how the environment and genetics influence structure.

- Gain a better understanding of what tools humans have developed to genetically alter organisms for human benefit.

The *STEM Road Map Curriculum Series* is anchored in the Next Generation Science Standards, the Common Core State Standards, and the Framework for 21st Century Learning. In-depth and flexible, *Genetically Modified Organisms* can be used as a whole unit or in part to meet the needs of districts, schools, and teachers who are charting a course toward an integrated STEM approach.

Carla C. Johnson is Professor of Science Education in the College of Education and Office of Research and Innovation, and a Faculty Research Fellow at North Carolina State University in North Carolina, USA

Janet B. Walton is Senior Research Scholar at North Carolina State University in North Carolina, USA

Erin E. Peters-Burton is the Donna R. and David E. Sterling Endowed Professor in Science Education at George Mason University in Virginia, USA

STEM ROAD MAP CURRICULUM SERIES

Series editors: Carla C. Johnson, Janet B. Walton, and Erin E. Peters-Burton

Map out a journey that will steer your students toward authentic problem solving as you ground them in integrated STEM disciplines.

Co-published by Routledge and NSTA Press, in partnership with the National Science Teaching Association, this K–12 curriculum series is anchored in the Next Generation Science Standards, the Common Core State Standards, and the Framework for 21st Century Learning. It was developed to meet the growing need to infuse real-world STEM learning into classrooms.

Each book is an in-depth module that uses project- and problem-based learning. First, your students are presented with a challenge. Then, they apply what they learn using science, social studies, English language arts, and mathematics. Engaging and flexible, each volume can be used as a whole unit or in part to meet the needs of districts, schools, and teachers who are charting a course toward an integrated STEM approach.

Modules are available from NSTA Press and Routledge, and organized under the following themes. For an update listing of the volumes in the series, please visit https://www.routledge.com/STEM-Road-Map-Curriculum-Series/book-series/SRM (for titles co-published by Routledge and NSTA Press), or www.nsta.org/book-series/stem-road-map-curriculum (for titles published by NSTA Press).

Co-published by Routledge and NSTA Press:

Optimizing the Human Experience:

- *Our Changing Environment, Grade K: STEM Road Map for Elementary School*
- *Genetically Modified Organisms, Grade 7: STEM Road Map for Middle School*
- *Rebuilding the Natural Environment, Grade 10: STEM Road Map for High School*
- *Mineral Resources, Grade 11: STEM Road Map for High School*

Cause and Effect:

- *Formation of the Earth, Grade 9: STEM Road Map for High School*

Published by NSTA Press:

Innovation and Progress:

- *Amusement Park of the Future, Grade 6: STEM Road Map for Elementary School*
- *Transportation in the Future, Grade 3: STEM Road Map for Elementary School*
- *Harnessing Solar Energy, Grade 4: STEM Road Map for Elementary School*
- *Wind Energy, Grade 5: STEM Road Map for Elementary School*
- *Construction Materials, Grade 11: STEM Road Map for High School*

The Represented World:

- *Patterns and the Plant World, Grade 1: STEM Road Map for Elementary School*

- *Investigating Environmental Changes, Grade 2: STEM Road Map for Elementary School*
- *Swing Set Makeover, Grade 3: STEM Road Map for Elementary School*
- *Rainwater Analysis, Grade 5: STEM Road Map for Elementary School*
- *Packaging Design, Grade 6: STEM Road Map for Middle School*
- *Improving Bridge Design, Grade 8: STEM Road Map for Middle School*
- *Radioactivity, Grade 11: STEM Road Map for High School*
- *Car Crashes, Grade 12: STEM Road Map for High School*

Cause and Effect:

- *Physics in Motion, Grade K: STEM Road Map for Elementary School*
- *Influence of Waves, Grade 1: STEM Road Map for Elementary School*
- *Natural Hazards, Grade 2: STEM Road Map for Elementary School*
- *Human Impacts on Our Climate, Grade 6: STEM Road Map for Middle School*
- *The Changing Earth, Grade 8: STEM Road Map for Middle School*
- *Healthy Living, Grade 10: STEM Road Map for High School*

Genetically Modified Organisms

Grade 7

STEM Road Map for Middle School

Edited by Carla C. Johnson, Janet B. Walton, and
Erin E. Peters-Burton

Routledge
Taylor & Francis Group

NEW YORK AND LONDON

nsta Press
National Science Teaching Association

Cover images: icon © Shutterstock, map © Getty Images
Art and design for cover and interior adapted from NSTA Press

First published 2022
by Routledge
605 Third Avenue, New York, NY 10158

and by Routledge
4 Park Square, Milton Park, Abingdon, Oxon, OX14 4RN

Routledge is an imprint of the Taylor & Francis Group, an informa business

A co-publication with NSTA Press.

Routledge is committed to publishing material that promotes the best in inquiry-based science education. However, conditions of actual use may vary, and the safety procedures and practices described in this book are intended to serve only as a guide. Additional precautionary measures may be required. Routledge and the authors do not warrant or represent that the procedures and practices in this book meet any safety code or standard of federal, state, or local regulations. Routledge and the authors disclaim any liability for personal injury or damage to property arising out of or relating to the use of this book, including any of the recommendations, instructions, or materials contained therein.

Trademark notice: Product or corporate names may be trademarks or registered trademarks, and are used only for identification and explanation without intent to infringe.

Library of Congress Cataloging-in-Publication Data
Names: Johnson, Carla C., 1969– editor. | Walton, Janet B., 1968– editor. | Peters-Burton, Erin E., editor.
Title: Genetically modified organisms, grade 7 : STEM road map for middle school / edited by Carla C. Johnson, Janet B. Walton, and Erin E. Peters-Burton.
Description: New York, NY : Routledge, 2022. | Series: STEM road map curriculum series | Includes bibliographical references and index.
Identifiers: LCCN 2021053360 | ISBN 9781032199832 (hardcover) | ISBN 9781032199825 (paperback) | ISBN 9781003261735 (ebook)
Subjects: LCSH: Transgenic organisms—Study and teaching (Middle school) | Genetic engineering—Study and teaching (Middle school)
Classification: LCC QH442.6 .G469 2022 | DDC 660.65—dc23/eng/20211222
LC record available at https://lccn.loc.gov/2021053360

ISBN: 978-1-032-19983-2 (hbk)
ISBN: 978-1-032-19982-5 (pbk)
ISBN: 978-1-003-26173-5 (ebk)

DOI: 10.4324/9781003261735

Typeset in Palatino LT Std
by Apex CoVantage, LLC

CONTENTS

CONTENTS

ABOUT THE EDITORS AND AUTHORS

Dr. Carla C. Johnson is a Professor of Science Education and ORI Faculty Research Fellow at NC State University in Raleigh, North Carolina. Dr. Johnson served as the director of research and evaluation for the Department of Defense-funded Army Educational Outreach Program (AEOP), a global portfolio of STEM education programs, competitions, and apprenticeships. She has been a leader in STEM education for the past decade, serving as the director of STEM Centers, editor of the *School Science and Mathematics* journal, and lead researcher for the evaluation of Tennessee's Race to the Top–funded STEM portfolio. Dr. Johnson has published over 100 articles, books, book chapters, and curriculum books focused on STEM education. She is a former science and social studies teacher and was the recipient of the 2013 Outstanding Science Teacher Educator of the Year award from the Association for Science Teacher Education (ASTE), the 2012 Award for Excellence in Integrating Science and Mathematics from the School Science and Mathematics Association (SSMA), the 2014 award for best paper on Implications of Research for Educational Practice from ASTE, and the 2006 Outstanding Early Career Scholar Award from SSMA. Her research focuses on STEM education policy implementation, effective science teaching, and integrated STEM approaches.

Dr. Janet B. Walton is a Senior Research Scholar at NC State's College of Education in Raleigh, North Carolina. Formerly the STEM workforce program manager for Virginia's Region 2000 and founding director of the Future Focus Foundation, a nonprofit organization dedicated to enhancing the quality of STEM education in the region, she merges her economic development and education backgrounds to develop K–12 curricular materials that integrate real-life issues with sound cross-curricular content. Her research focus includes collaboration between schools and community stakeholders for STEM education, problem- and project- based learning pedagogies, online learning, and mixed methods research methodologies. She leverages this background to bring contextual STEM experiences into the classroom and provide students and educators with innovative resources and curricular materials. She is the former assistant director of evaluation of research and evaluation for the Department of Defense-funded Army Educational Outreach Program (AEOP), a global portfolio of STEM education programs, competitions, and apprenticeships and specializes in evaluation of STEM programs.

Dr. Erin E. Peters-Burton is the Donna R. and David E. Sterling Endowed Professor in Science Education at George Mason University in Fairfax, Virginia. She uses her experiences from 15 years as an engineer and secondary science, engineering, and mathematics teacher to develop research projects that directly inform classroom practice in science and engineering. Her research agenda is based on the idea that all students should build self-awareness of how they learn science and engineering. She works to help students see themselves as "science- minded" and help teachers create classrooms that support student skills to develop scientific knowledge. To accomplish this, she pursues research projects that investigate ways that students and teachers can use self-regulated learning theory in science and engineering, as well as how inclusive STEM schools can help students succeed. She received the Outstanding Science Teacher Educator of the Year award from ASTE in 2016 and a Teacher of Distinction Award and a Scholarly Achievement Award from George Mason University in 2012, and in 2010 she was named University Science Educator of the Year by the Virginia Association of Science Teachers.

Dr. Tamara J. Moore is an associate professor of engineering education in the College of Engineering at Purdue University. Dr. Moore's research focuses on defining STEM integration through the use of engineering as the connection and investigating its power for student learning.

Dr. Toni A. May is an associate professor of assessment, research, and statistics in the School of Education at Drexel University in Philadelphia. Dr. May's research concentrates on assessment and evaluation in education, with a focus on K–12 STEM.

Dr. Stephen Burton is the Science Outreach Teacher for Loudoun County Public Schools in Virginia. He also is an adjunct instructor for science education at George Mason University in Fairfax, VA.

ACKNOWLEDGMENTS

This module was developed as a part of the STEM Road Map project (Carla C. Johnson, principal investigator). The Purdue University College of Education, General Motors, and other sources provided funding for this project.

See *www.routledge.com/9781138804234* for more information about *STEM Road Map: A Framework for Integrated STEM Education*.

PART 1

THE STEM ROAD MAP

BACKGROUND, THEORY, AND PRACTICE

OVERVIEW OF THE *STEM ROAD MAP CURRICULUM SERIES*

Carla C. Johnson, Erin E. Peters-Burton, and Tamara J. Moore

The *STEM Road Map Curriculum Series* was conceptualized and developed by a team of STEM educators from across the United States in response to a growing need to infuse real-world learning contexts, delivered through authentic problem-solving pedagogy, into K–12 classrooms. The curriculum series is grounded in integrated STEM, which focuses on the integration of the STEM disciplines – science, technology, engineering, and mathematics – delivered across content areas, incorporating the Framework for 21st Century Learning along with grade-level-appropriate academic standards. The curriculum series begins in kindergarten, with a five-week instructional sequence that introduces students to the STEM themes and gives them grade-level-appropriate topics and real-world challenges or problems to solve. The series uses project-based and problem-based learning, presenting students with the problem or challenge during the first lesson, and then teaching them science, social studies, English language arts, mathematics, and other content, as they apply what they learn to the challenge or problem at hand.

Authentic assessment and differentiation are embedded throughout the modules. Each *STEM Road Map Curriculum Series* module has a lead discipline, which may be science, social studies, English language arts, or mathematics. All disciplines are integrated into each module, along with ties to engineering. Another key component is the use of STEM Research Notebooks to allow students to track their own learning progress. The modules are designed with a scaffolded approach, with increasingly complex concepts and skills introduced as students' progress through grade levels.

The developers of this work view the curriculum as a resource that is intended to be used either as a whole or in part to meet the needs of districts, schools, and teachers who are implementing an integrated STEM approach. A variety of implementation formats are possible, from using one stand- alone module at a given grade level to using all five modules to provide 25 weeks of instruction. Also, within each grade

DOI: 10.4324/9781003261735-2

band (K– 2, 3–5, 6–8, 9–12), the modules can be sequenced in various ways to suit specific needs.

STANDARDS-BASED APPROACH

The *STEM Road Map Curriculum Series* is anchored in the *Next Generation Science Standards (NGSS)*, the *Common Core State Standards for Mathematics (CCSS Mathematics)*, the *Common Core State Standards for English Language Arts (CCSS ELA)*, and the Framework for 21st Century Learning. Each module includes a detailed curriculum map that incorporates the associated standards from the particular area correlated to lesson plans. The STEM Road Map has very clear and strong connections to these academic standards, and each of the grade-level topics was derived from the mapping of the standards to ensure alignment among topics, challenges or problems, and the required academic standards for students. Therefore, the curriculum series takes a standards-based approach and is designed to provide authentic contexts for application of required knowledge and skills.

THEMES IN THE *STEM ROAD MAP CURRICULUM SERIES*

The K–12 STEM Road Map is organized around five real-world STEM themes that were generated through an examination of the big ideas and challenges for society included in STEM standards and those that are persistent dilemmas for current and future generations:

- Cause and Effect
- Innovation and Progress
- The Represented World
- Sustainable Systems
- Optimizing the Human Experience

These themes are designed as springboards for launching students into an exploration of real-world learning situated within big ideas. Most important, the five STEM Road Map themes serve as a framework for scaffolding STEM learning across the K–12 continuum.

The themes are distributed across the STEM disciplines so that they represent the big ideas in science (Cause and Effect; Sustainable Systems), technology (Innovation and Progress; Optimizing the Human Experience), engineering (Innovation and Progress; Sustainable Systems; Optimizing the Human Experience), and mathematics (The Rep- resented World), as well as concepts and challenges in social studies and 21st century skills that are also excellent contexts for learning in English language arts. The process of developing themes began with the clustering of the *NGSS* performance expectations and the National Academy of Engineering's grand challenges for engineering, which led to the development of the challenge in each module and connections of the module activities to the *CCSS Mathematics* and *CCSS ELA* standards. We performed these mapping processes with large teams of experts and found that these five themes pro- vided breadth, depth, and coherence to frame a high-quality STEM learning experience from kindergarten through 12th grade.

Cause and Effect

The concept of cause and effect is a powerful and pervasive notion in the STEM fields. It is the foundation of understanding how and why things happen as they do. Humans spend considerable effort and resources trying to understand the causes and effects of natural and designed phenomena to gain better control over events and the environment and to be prepared to react appropriately. Equipped with the knowledge of a specific cause-and-effect relationship, we can lead better lives or contribute to the community by altering the cause, leading to a different effect. For example, if a person recognizes that irresponsible energy consumption leads to global climate change, that person can act to remedy his or her contribution to the situation. Although cause and effect is a core idea in the STEM fields, it can actually be difficult to determine. Students should be capable of understanding not only when evidence points to cause and effect but also when evidence points to relationships but not direct causality. The major goal of education is to foster students to be empowered, analytic thinkers, capable of thinking through complex processes to make important decisions. Understanding causality, as well as when it cannot be determined, will help students become better consumers, global citizens, and community members.

Innovation and Progress

One of the most important factors in determining whether humans will have a positive future is innovation. Innovation is the driving force behind progress, which helps create possibilities that did not exist before. Innovation and progress are creative entities, but in the STEM fields, they are anchored by evidence and logic, and they use established concepts to move the STEM fields forward. In creating something new, students must consider what is already known in the STEM fields and apply this knowledge appropriately. When we innovate, we create value that was not there previously and create new conditions and possibilities for even more innovations. Students should consider how their innovations might affect progress and use their STEM thinking to change current human burdens to benefits. For example, if we develop more efficient cars that use by-products from another manufacturing industry, such as food processing, then we have used waste productively and reduced the need for the waste to be hauled away, an indirect benefit of the innovation.

The Represented World

When we communicate about the world we live in, how the world works, and how we can meet the needs of humans, sometimes we can use the actual phenomena to explain a concept. Sometimes, however, the concept is too big, too slow, too small, too fast, or too complex for us to explain using the actual phenomena, and we must use a representation or a model to help communicate the important features. We need representations and models such as graphs, tables, mathematical expressions, and diagrams because it makes our thinking visible. For example, when examining geologic time, we cannot actually observe the passage of such large chunks of time, so we create a timeline or a model that uses a proportional scale to visually illustrate how much time has passed for different eras. Another example may be something too complex for students at a particular grade level, such as explaining the p subshell orbitals of electrons to fifth graders. Instead, we use the Bohr model, which more closely represents the orbiting of planets and is accessible to fifth graders.

When we create models, they are helpful because they point out the most important features of a phenomenon. We also create representations of the world with mathematical functions, which help us change parameters to suit the situation. Creating representations of a phenomenon engages students because they are able to identify the important features of that phenomenon and communicate them directly. But because models are estimates of a phenomenon, they leave out some of the details, so it is important for students to evaluate their usefulness as well as their shortcomings.

Sustainable Systems

From an engineering perspective, the term *system* refers to the use of "concepts of component need, component interaction, systems interaction, and feedback. The interaction of subcomponents to produce a functional system is a common lens used by all engineering disciplines for understanding, analysis, and design." (Koehler, Bloom, and Binns 2013, p. 8). Systems can be either open (e.g., an ecosystem) or closed (e.g., a car battery). Ideally, a system should be sustainable, able to maintain equilibrium without much energy from outside the structure. Looking at a garden, we see flowers blooming, weeds sprouting, insects buzzing, and various forms of life living within its boundaries. This is an example of an ecosystem, a collection of living organisms that survive together, functioning as a system. The interaction of the organisms within the system and the influences of the environment (e.g., water, sunlight) can maintain the system for a period of time, thus demonstrating its ability to endure. Sustainability is a desirable feature of a system because it allows for existence of the entity in the long term.

In the STEM Road Map project, we identified different standards that we consider to be oriented toward systems that students should know and understand in the K–12 setting. These include ecosystems, the rock cycle, Earth processes (such as erosion, tectonics, ocean currents, weather phenomena), Earth-Sun-Moon cycles, heat transfer, and the interaction among the geosphere, biosphere, hydrosphere, and atmosphere. Stu- dents and teachers should understand that we live in a world of systems that are not independent of each other, but rather are intrinsically linked such that a disruption in one part of a system will have reverberating effects on other parts of the system.

Optimizing the Human Experience

Science, technology, engineering, and mathematics as disciplines have the capacity to continuously improve the ways humans live, interact, and find meaning in the world, thus working to optimize the human experience. This idea has two components: being more suited to our environment and being more fully human. For example, the pro- gression of STEM ideas can help humans create solutions to complex problems, such as improving ways to access water sources, designing energy sources with minimal impact on our environment, developing new ways of communication and expres- sion, and building efficient shelters. STEM ideas can also provide access to the secrets and wonders of nature. Learning in STEM requires students to think logically and systematically, which is a way of knowing the world that is markedly different from knowing the world as an artist. When students can employ various ways of know- ing and understand when it is appropriate to use a different way of knowing or inte- grate ways of knowing, they are fully experiencing the best of what it is to be human. The problem-based learning scenarios provided in the STEM Road Map help students develop ways of thinking like STEM professionals as they ask questions and design solutions. They learn to optimize the human experience by innovating improvements in the designed world in which they live.

THE NEED FOR AN INTEGRATED STEM APPROACH

At a basic level, STEM stands for science, technology, engineering, and mathematics. Over the past decade, however, STEM has evolved to have a much broader scope and implications. Now, educators and policy makers refer to STEM as not only a concen- trated area for investing in the future of the United States and other nations but also as a domain and mechanism for educational reform. The good intentions of the recent decade-plus of focus on accountability and increased testing has resulted in significant decreases not only in instructional time for teaching science and social studies but also in the flexibility of teachers to promote authentic, problem solving–focused classroom environments. The shift has had a detrimental impact on student acquisition of vitally important skills, which many refer to as 21st century skills, and often the ability of stu- dents to "think." Further, schooling has become increasingly siloed into compartments of mathematics, science, English language, arts and social studies, lacking any of the

connections that are overwhelmingly present in the real world around children. Students have experienced school as content provided in boxes that must be memorized, devoid of any real-world context, and often have little understanding of why they are learning these things.

STEM-focused projects, curriculum, activities, and schools have emerged as a means to address these challenges. However, most of these efforts have continued to focus on the individual STEM disciplines (predominantly science and engineering) through more STEM classes and after-school programs in a "STEM enhanced" approach (Breiner et al. 2012). But in traditional and STEM enhanced approaches, there is little to no focus on other disciplines that are integral to the context of STEM in the real world. Integrated STEM education, on the other hand, infuses the learning of important STEM content and concepts with a much-needed emphasis on 21st century skills and a problem- and project-based pedagogy that more closely mirrors the real-world setting for society's challenges. It incorporates social studies, English language arts, and the arts as pivotal and necessary (Johnson 2013; Rennie, Venville, and Wallace 2012; Roehrig et al. 2012).

Framework for Stem Integration in The Classroom

The *STEM Road Map Curriculum Series* is grounded in the Framework for STEM Integration in the Classroom as conceptualized by Moore, Guzey, and Brown (2014) and Moore et al. (2014). The framework has six elements, described in the context of how they are used in the *STEM Road Map Curriculum Series* as follows:

1. The STEM Road Map contexts are meaningful to students and provide motivation to engage with the content. Together, these allow students to have different ways to enter into the challenge.

2. The STEM Road Map modules include engineering design that allows students to design technologies (i.e., products that are part of the designed world) for a compelling purpose.

3. The STEM Road Map modules provide students with the opportunities to learn from failure and redesign based on the lessons learned.

4. The STEM Road Map modules include standards-based disciplinary content as the learning objectives.

5. The STEM Road Map modules include student-centered pedagogies that allow students to grapple with the content, tie their ideas to the context, and learn to think for themselves as they deepen their conceptual knowledge.

6. The STEM Road Map modules emphasize 21st century skills and, in particular, highlight communication and teamwork.

All of the STEM Road Map modules incorporate these six elements; however, the level of emphasis on each of these elements varies based on the challenge or problem in each module.

THE NEED FOR THE *STEM ROAD MAP CURRICULUM SERIES*

As focus is increasing on integrated STEM, and additional schools and programs decide to move their curriculum and instruction in this direction, there is a need for high- quality, research-based curriculum designed with integrated STEM at the core. Several good resources are available to help teachers infuse engineering or more STEM enhanced approaches, but no curriculum exists that spans K–12 with an integrated STEM focus. The next chapter provides detailed information about the specific pedagogy, instructional strategies, and learning theory on which the *STEM Road Map Curriculum Series* is grounded.

REFERENCES

Breiner, J., M. Harkness, C. C. Johnson, and C. Koehler. 2012. What is STEM? A discussion about conceptions of STEM in education and partnerships. *School Science and Mathematics* 112 (1): 3–11.

Johnson, C. C. 2013. Conceptualizing integrated STEM education: Editorial. *School Science and Mathematics* 113 (8): 367–368.

Koehler, C. M., M. A. Bloom, and I. C. Binns. 2013. Lights, camera, action: Developing a methodology to document mainstream films' portrayal of nature of science and scientific inquiry. *Electronic Journal of Science Education* 17 (2).

Moore, T. J., S. S. Guzey, and A. Brown. 2014. Greenhouse design to increase habitable land: An engineering unit. *Science Scope* 51–57.

Moore, T. J., M. S. Stohlmann, H.-H. Wang, K. M. Tank, A. W. Glancy, and G. H. Roehrig. 2014. Implementation and integration of engineering in K–12 STEM education. In *Engineering in pre- college settings: Synthesizing research, policy, and practices,* ed. S. Purzer, J. Strobel, and M. Cardella, 35–60. West Lafayette, IN: Purdue Press.

Rennie, L., G. Venville, and J. Wallace. 2012. *Integrating science, technology, engineering, and mathematics: Issues, reflections, and ways forward.* New York: Routledge.

Roehrig, G. H., T. J. Moore, H. H. Wang, and M. S. Park. 2012. Is adding the E enough? Investigating the impact of K–12 engineering standards on the implementation of STEM integration. *School Science and Mathematics* 112 (1): 31–44.

STRATEGIES USED IN THE *STEM ROAD MAP CURRICULUM SERIES*

Erin E. Peters-Burton, Carla C. Johnson, Toni A. May, and Tamara J. Moore

The *STEM Road Map Curriculum Series* uses what has been identified through research as best-practice pedagogy, including embedded formative assessment strategies throughout each module. This chapter briefly describes the key strategies that are employed in the series.

PROJECT- AND PROBLEM-BASED LEARNING

Each module in the *STEM Road Map Curriculum Series* uses either project-based learning or problem-based learning to drive the instruction. Project-based learning begins with a driving question to guide student teams in addressing a contextualized local or community problem or issue. The outcome of project-based instruction is a product that is conceptualized, designed, and tested through a series of scaffolded learning experiences (Blumenfeld et al. 1991; Krajcik and Blumenfeld 2006). Problem-based learning is often grounded in a fictitious scenario, challenge, or problem (Barell 2006; Lambros 2004). On the first day of instruction within the unit, student teams are provided with the context of the problem. Teams work through a series of activities and use open-ended research to develop their potential solution to the problem or challenge, which need not be a tangible product (Johnson 2003).

ENGINEERING DESIGN PROCESS

The *STEM Road Map Curriculum Series* uses engineering design as a way to facilitate integrated STEM within the modules. The engineering design process (EDP) is depicted in Figure 2.1 (p. 10). It highlights two major aspects of engineering design – problem scoping and solution generation – and six specific components of

DOI: 10.4324/9781003261735-3

Figure 2.1. Engineering Design Process

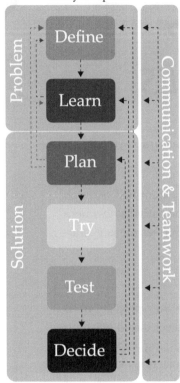

Copyright © 2015 PictureSTEM-Purdue University Research Foundation

working toward a design: define the problem, learn about the problem, plan a solution, try the solution, test the solution, decide whether the solution is good enough. It also shows that communication and teamwork are involved throughout the entire process. As the arrows in the figure indicate, the order in which the components of engineering design are addressed depends on what becomes needed as designers progress through the EDP. Designers must communicate and work in teams throughout the process. The EDP is iterative, meaning that components of the process can be repeated as needed until the design is good enough to present to the client as a potential solution to the problem.

Problem scoping is the process of gathering and analyzing information to deeply understand the engineering design problem. It includes defining the problem and learning about the problem. Defining the problem includes identifying the problem, the client, and the end user of the design. The client is the person (or people) who hired the designers to do the work, and the end user is the person (or people) who will use the final design. The designers must also identify the criteria and the constraints of the problem. The criteria are the things the client wants from the solution, and the constraints are the things that limit the possible solutions. The designers must spend significant time learning about the problem, which can include activities such as the following:

- Reading informational texts and researching about relevant concepts or contexts

- Identifying and learning about needed mathematical and scientific skills, knowledge, and tools

- Learning about things done previously to solve similar problems

- Experimenting with possible materials that could be used in the design

Problem scoping also allows designers to consider how to measure the success of the design in addressing specific criteria and staying within the constraints over multiple iterations of solution generation.

Solution generation includes planning a solution, trying the solution, testing the solution, and deciding whether the solution is good enough. Planning the solution includes generating many design ideas that both address the criteria and meet the constraints.

Here the designers must consider what was learned about the problem during problem scoping. Design plans include clear communication of design ideas through media such as notebooks, blueprints, schematics, or storyboards. They also include details about the design, such as measurements, materials, colors, costs of materials, instructions for how things fit together, and sets of directions. Making the decision about which design idea to move forward involves considering the trade-offs of each design idea.

Once a clear design plan is in place, the designers must try the solution. Trying the solution includes developing a prototype (a testable model) based on the plan generated. The prototype might be something physical or a process to accomplish a goal. This component of design requires that the designers consider the risk involved in implementing the design. The prototype developed must be tested. Testing the solution includes conducting fair tests that verify whether the plan is a solution that is good enough to meet the client and end user needs and wants. Data need to be collected about the results of the tests of the prototype, and these data should be used to make evidence-based decisions regarding the design choices made in the plan. Here, the designers must again consider the criteria and constraints for the problem.

Using the data gathered from the testing, the designers must decide whether the solution is good enough to meet the client and end user needs and wants by assessment based on the criteria and constraints. Here, the designers must justify or reject design decisions based on the background research gathered while learning about the problem and on the evidence gathered during the testing of the solution. The designers must now decide whether to present the current solution to the client as a possibility or to do more iterations of design on the solution. If they decide that improvements need to be made to the solution, the designers must decide if there is more that needs to be understood about the problem, client, or end user; if another design idea should be tried; or if more planning needs to be conducted on the same design. One way or another, more work needs to be done.

Throughout the process of designing a solution to meet a client's needs and wants, designers work in teams and must communicate to each other, the client, and likely the end user. Teamwork is important in engineering design because multiple perspectives and differing skills and knowledge are valuable when working to solve problems. Communication is key to the success of the designed solution. Designers must communicate their ideas clearly using many different representations, such as text in an engineering notebook, diagrams, flowcharts, technical briefs, or memos to the client.

LEARNING CYCLE

The same format for the learning cycle is used in all grade levels throughout the STEM Road Map, so that students engage in a variety of activities to learn about phenomena in the modules thoroughly and have consistent experiences in the problem- and project-based learning modules. Expectations for learning by younger students are

not as high as for older students, but the format of the progression of learning is the same. Students who have learned with curriculum from the STEM Road Map in early grades know what to expect in later grades. The learning cycle consists of five parts – Introductory Activity/Engagement, Activity/Exploration, Explanation, Elaboration/ Application of Knowledge, and Evaluation/Assessment – and is based on the empirically tested 5E model from BSCS (Bybee et al. 2006).

In the Introductory Activity/Engagement phase, teachers introduce the module challenge and use a unique approach designed to pique students' curiosity. This phase gets students to start thinking about what they already know about the topic and begin wondering about key ideas. The Introductory Activity/Engagement phase positions students to be confident about what they are about to learn, because they have prior knowledge, and clues them into what they don't yet know.

In the Activity/Exploration phase, the teacher sets up activities in which students experience a deeper look at the topics that were introduced earlier. Students engage in the activities and generate new questions or consider possibilities using preliminary investigations. Students work independently, in small groups, and in whole-group settings to conduct investigations, resulting in common experiences about the topic and skills involved in the real-world activities. Teachers can assess students' development of concepts and skills based on the common experiences during this phase.

During the Explanation phase, teachers direct students' attention to concepts they need to understand and skills they need to possess to accomplish the challenge. Students participate in activities to demonstrate their knowledge and skills to this point, and teachers can pinpoint gaps in student knowledge during this phase.

In the Elaboration/Application of Knowledge phase, teachers present students with activities that engage in higher-order thinking to create depth and breadth of student knowledge, while connecting ideas across topics within and across STEM. Students apply what they have learned thus far in the module to a new context or elaborate on what they have learned about the topic to a deeper level of detail.

In the last phase, Evaluation/Assessment, teachers give students summative feedback on their knowledge and skills as demonstrated through the challenge. This is not the only point of assessment (as discussed in the section on Embedded Formative Assessments), but it is an assessment of the culmination of the knowledge and skills for the module. Students demonstrate their cognitive growth at this point and reflect on how far they have come since the beginning of the module. The challenges are designed to be multidimensional in the ways students must collaborate and communicate their new knowledge.

STEM RESEARCH NOTEBOOK

One of the main components of the *STEM Road Map Curriculum Series* is the STEM Research Notebook, a place for students to capture their ideas, questions, observations, reflections, evidence of progress, and other items associated with their daily work. At the beginning of each module, the teacher walks students through the setup of the STEM Research Notebook, which could be a three-ring binder, composition book, or spiral notebook. You may wish to have students create divided sections so that they can easily access work from various disciplines during the module. Electronic notebooks kept on student devices are also acceptable and encouraged. Students will develop their own table of contents and create chapters in the notebook for each module.

Each lesson in the *STEM Road Map Curriculum Series* includes one or more prompts that are designed for inclusion in the STEM Research Notebook and appear as questions or statements that the teacher assigns to students. These prompts require students to apply what they have learned across the lesson to solve the big problem or challenge for that module. Each lesson is designed to meaningfully refer students to the larger problem or challenge they have been assigned to solve with their teams. The STEM Research Notebook is designed to be a key formative assessment tool, as students' daily entries provide evidence of what they are learning. The notebook can be used as a mechanism for dialogue between the teacher and students, as well as for peer and self-evaluation.

The use of the STEM Research Notebook is designed to scaffold student notebooking skills across the grade bands in the *STEM Road Map Curriculum Series*. In the early grades, children learn how to organize their daily work in the notebook as a way to collect their products for future reference. In elementary school, students structure their notebooks to integrate background research along with their daily work and lesson prompts. In the upper grades (middle and high school), students expand their use of research and data gathering through team discussions to more closely mirror the work of STEM experts in the real world.

THE ROLE OF ASSESSMENT IN THE *STEM ROAD MAP CURRICULUM SERIES*

Starting in the middle years and continuing into secondary education, the word *assessment* typically brings grades to mind. These grades may take the form of a letter or a percentage, but they typically are used as a representation of a student's content mastery. If well thought out and implemented, however, classroom assessment can offer teachers, parents, and students valuable information about student learning and misconceptions that does not necessarily come in the form of a grade (Popham 2013).

The *STEM Road Map Curriculum Series* provides a set of assessments for each module. Teachers are encouraged to use assessment information for more than just assigning grades to students. Instead, assessments of activities requiring students to actively engage in their learning, such as student journaling in STEM Research Notebooks, collaborative presentations, and constructing graphic organizers, should be used to move student learning forward. Whereas other curriculum with assessments may include

objective-type (multiple-choice or matching) tests, quizzes, or worksheets, we have intentionally avoided these forms of assessments to better align assessment strategies with teacher instruction and student learning techniques. Since the focus of this book is on project- or problem-based STEM curriculum and instruction that focuses on higher-level thinking skills, appropriate and authentic performance assessments were developed to elicit the most reliable and valid indication of growth in student abilities (Brookhart and Nitko 2008).

Comprehensive Assessment System

Assessment throughout all STEM Road Map curriculum modules acts as a comprehensive system in which formative and summative assessments work together to provide teachers with high-quality information on student learning. Formative assessment occurs when the teacher finds out formally or informally what a student knows about a smaller, defined concept or skill and provides timely feedback to the student about his or her level of proficiency. Summative assessments occur when students have performed all activities in the module and are given a cumulative performance evaluation in which they demonstrate their growth in learning.

A comprehensive assessment system can be thought of as akin to a sporting event. Formative assessments are the practices: It is important to accomplish them consistently, they provide feedback to help students improve their learning, and making mistakes can be worthwhile if students are given an opportunity to learn from them. Summative assessments are the competitions: Students need to be prepared to perform at the best of their ability. Without multiple opportunities to practice skills along the way through formative assessments, students will not have the best chance of demonstrating growth in abilities through summative assessments (Black and Wiliam 1998).

Embedded Formative Assessments

Formative assessments in this module serve two main purposes: to provide feedback to students about their learning and to provide important information for the teacher to inform immediate instructional needs. Providing feedback to students is particularly important when conducting problem- or project-based learning because students take on much of the responsibility for learning, and teachers must facilitate student learning in an informed way. For example, if students are required to conduct research for the Activity/Exploration phase but are not familiar with what constitutes a reliable resource, they may develop misconceptions based on poor information. When a teacher monitors this learning through formative assessments and provides specific feedback related to the instructional goals, students are less likely to develop incomplete or incorrect conceptions in their independent investigations. By using formative assessment to detect problems in student learning and then acting on this information, teachers help move student learning forward through these teachable moments.

Formative assessments come in a variety of formats. They can be informal, such as asking students probing questions related to student knowledge or tasks or simply observing students engaged in an activity to gather information about student skills. Formative assessments can also be formal, such as a written quiz or a laboratory practical.

Regardless of the type, three key steps must be completed when using formative assessments (Sondergeld, Bell, and Leusner 2010). First, the assessment is delivered to students so that teachers can collect data. Next, teachers analyze the data (student responses) to determine student strengths and areas that need additional support. Finally, teachers use the results from information collected to modify lessons and create learning environments that reinforce weak points in student learning. If student learning information is not used to modify instruction, the assessment cannot be considered formative in nature. Formative assessments can be about content, science process skills, or even learning skills. When a formative assessment focuses on content, it assesses student knowledge about the disciplinary core ideas from the *Next Generation Science Standards* (*NGSS*) or content objectives from *Common Core State Standards for Mathematics* (*CCSS Mathematics*) or *Common Core State Standards for English Language Arts* (*CCSS ELA*). Content-focused formative assessments ask students questions about declarative knowledge regarding the concepts they have been learning. Process skills formative assessments examine the extent to which a student can perform science and engineering practices from the *NGSS* or process objectives from *CCSS Mathematics* or *CCSS ELA*, such as constructing an argument. Learning skills can also be assessed formatively by asking students to reflect on the ways they learn best during a module and identify ways they could have learned more.

Assessment Maps

Assessment maps or blueprints can be used to ensure alignment between classroom instruction and assessment. If what students are learning in the classroom is not the same as the content on which they are assessed, the resultant judgment made on student learning will be invalid (Brookhart and Nitko 2008). Therefore, the issue of instruction and assessment alignment is critical. The assessment map for this book (found in Chapter 3) indicates by lesson whether the assessment should be completed as a group or on an individual basis, identifies the assessment as formative or summative in nature, and aligns the assessment with its corresponding learning objectives.

Note that the module includes far more formative assessments than summative assessments. This is done intentionally to provide students with multiple opportunities to practice their learning of new skills before completing a summative assessment. Note also that formative assessments are used to collect information on only one or two learning objectives at a time so that potential relearning or instructional modifications can focus on smaller and more manageable chunks of information. Conversely,

summative assessments in the module cover many more learning objectives, as they are traditionally used as final markers of student learning. This is not to say that information collected from summative assessments cannot or should not be used formatively. If teachers find that gaps in student learning persist after a summative assessment is completed, it is important to revisit these existing misconceptions or areas of weakness before moving on (Black et al. 2003).

SELF-REGULATED LEARNING THEORY IN THE STEM ROAD MAP MODULES

Many learning theories are compatible with the STEM Road Map modules, such as constructivism, situated cognition, and meaningful learning. However, we feel that the self-regulated learning theory (SRL) aligns most appropriately (Zimmerman 2000). SRL requires students to understand that thinking needs to be motivated and managed (Ritchhart, Church, and Morrison 2011). The STEM Road Map modules are student centered and are designed to provide students with choices, concrete hands-on experiences, and opportunities to see and make connections, especially across subjects (Eliason and Jenkins 2012; NAEYC 2016). Additionally, SRL is compatible with the modules because it fosters a learning environment that supports students' motivation, enables students to become aware of their own learning strategies, and requires reflection on learning while experiencing the module (Peters and Kitsantas 2010).

The theory behind SRL (see Figure 2.2) explains the different processes that students engage in before, during, and after a learning task. Because SRL is a cyclical learning process, the accomplishment of one cycle develops strategies for the next learning cycle. This cyclic way of learning aligns with the various sections in the STEM Road Map lesson plans on Introductory Activity/ Engagement, Activity/ Exploration, Explanation, Elaboration/Application of Knowledge, and Evaluation/Assessment. Since the students engaged in a module take on much of the responsibility for learning, this theory also provides guidance for teachers to keep students on the right track.

Figure 2.2. SRL Theory

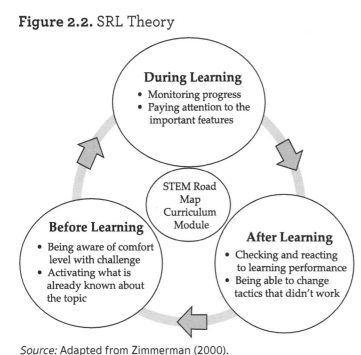

Source: Adapted from Zimmerman (2000).

Table 2.1. SRL Learning Process Components

Learning Process Components	Example from Rebuilding the Natural Environment Module	Lesson Number
Before Learning		
Motivates students	Students brainstorm their own experiences with energy consumption.	Lesson 1
Evokes prior learning	Students will discuss their understanding of electricity generation within teams and share their ideas with the class. Students will be asked to give their responses on the following questions: (a) What is electricity? (b) How is it generated? (c) How does it get to our houses?	Lesson 1
During Learning		
Focuses on important features	Students must determine the cost-effectiveness of taking a single-family home off the current electrical grid and powering it solely from available renewable/sustainable energy sources. Students will need to research the energy output of devices, use weather data to accurately estimate the amount of time each device will be able to generate electricity (amount of sunlight per day and season for solar, average amount of wind per day and season for wind, etc.), and conservatively calculate the kilowatt hours generated on average for a whole-home system.	Lesson 3
Helps students monitor their progress	Teacher monitors student STEM Research Notebooks for the accuracy of each device and for how the devices work as a system.	Lesson 3
After Learning		
Evaluates learning	Students receive feedback on the rubric for their innovation for their group work and for their individual work.	Lesson 4
Takes account of what worked and what did not work	Students will write a reflection on the quality of their work given feedback from the class and teacher.	Lesson 4

The remainder of this section explains how SRL theory is embedded within the five sections of each module and points out ways to support students in becoming independent learners of STEM while productively functioning in collaborative teams.

Before Learning: Setting the Stage

Before attempting a learning task such as the STEM Road Map modules, teachers should develop an understanding of their students' level of comfort with the process of accomplishing the learning and determine what they already know about the topic. When students are comfortable with attempting a learning task, they tend to take more risks in learning and as a result achieve deeper learning (Bandura 1986).

The STEM Road Map curriculum modules are designed to foster excitement from the very beginning. Each module has an Introductory Activity/Engagement section that introduces the overall topic from a unique and exciting perspective, engaging the students to learn more so that they can accomplish the challenge. The Introductory Activity also has a design component that helps teachers assess what students already know about the topic of the module. In addition to the deliberate designs in the lesson plans to support SRL, teachers can support a high level of student comfort with the learning challenge by finding out if students have ever accomplished the same kind of task and, if so, asking them to share what worked well for them.

During Learning: Staying the Course

Some students fear inquiry learning because they aren't sure what to do to be successful (Peters 2010). However, the STEM Road Map curriculum modules are embedded with tools to help students pay attention to knowledge and skills that are important for the learning task and to check student understanding along the way. One of the most important processes for learning is the ability for learners to monitor their own progress while performing a learning task (Peters 2012). The modules allow students to monitor their progress with tools such as the STEM Research Notebooks, in which they record what they know and can check whether they have acquired a complete set of knowledge and skills. The STEM Road Map modules support inquiry strategies that include previewing, questioning, predicting, clarifying, observing, discussing, and journaling (Morrison and Milner 2014). Through the use of technology throughout the modules, inquiry is supported by providing students access to resources and data while enabling them to process information, report the findings, collaborate, and develop 21st century skills.

It is important for teachers to encourage students to have an open mind about alternative solutions and procedures (Milner and Sondergeld 2015) when working through the STEM Road Map curriculum modules. Novice learners can have difficulty knowing what to pay attention to and tend to treat each possible avenue for information as equal (Benner 1984). Teachers are the mentors in a classroom and can point out ways for students to approach learning during the Activity/Exploration, Explanation, and Elaboration/Application of Knowledge portions of the lesson plans to ensure that students pay attention to the important concepts and skills throughout the module. For example, if a student is to demonstrate conceptual awareness of motion when working on roller coaster research, but the student has misconceptions about motion, the teacher can step in and redirect student learning.

After Learning: Knowing What Works

The classroom is a busy place, and it may often seem that there is no time for self-reflection on learning. Although skipping this reflective process may save time in the short term, it reduces the ability to take into account things that worked well and things that didn't so that teaching the module may be improved next time. In the long run, SRL skills are critical for students to become independent learners who can adapt to new situations. By investing the time it takes to teach students SRL skills, teachers can save time later, because students will be able to apply methods and approaches for learning that they have found effective to new situations. In the Evaluation/Assessment portion of the STEM Road Map curriculum modules, as well as in the formative assessments throughout the modules, two processes in the after-learning phase are supported: evaluating one's own performance and accounting for ways to adapt tactics that didn't work well. Students have many opportunities to self-assess in formative assessments, both in groups and individually, using the rubrics provided in the modules.

The designs of the *NGSS* and *CCSS* allow for students to learn in diverse ways, and the STEM Road Map curriculum modules emphasize that students can use a variety of tactics to complete the learning process. For example, students can use STEM Research Notebooks to record what they have learned during the various research activities. Notebook entries might include putting objectives in students' own words, compiling their prior learning on the topic, documenting new learning, providing proof of what they learned, and reflecting on what they felt successful doing and what they felt they still needed to work on. Perhaps students didn't realize that they were supposed to connect what they already knew with what they learned. They could record this and would be prepared in the next learning task to begin connecting prior learning with new learning.

SAFETY IN STEM

Student safety is a primary consideration in all subjects but is an area of particular concern in science, where students may interact with unfamiliar tools and materials that may pose additional safety risks. It is important to implement safety practices within the context of STEM investigations, whether in a classroom laboratory or in the field.

When you keep safety in mind as a teacher, you avoid many potential issues with the lesson while also protecting your students.

STEM safety practices encompass things considered in the typical science classroom. Ensure that students are familiar with basic safety considerations, such as wearing protective equipment (e.g., safety glasses or goggles and latex-free gloves) and taking care with sharp objects, and know emergency exit procedures. Teachers should learn beforehand the locations of the safety eyewash, fume hood, fire extinguishers, and emergency shut-off switch in the classroom and how to use them. Also be aware of any school or district safety policies that are in place and apply those that align with the work being conducted in the lesson. It is important to review all safety procedures annually.

STEM investigations should always be supervised. Each lesson in the modules includes teacher guidelines for applicable safety procedures that should be followed. Before each investigation, teachers should go over these safety procedures with the student teams. Some STEM focus areas such as engineering require that students can demonstrate how to properly use equipment in the maker space before the teacher allows them to proceed with the lesson.

Information about classroom science safety, including a safety checklist for science classrooms, general lab safety recommendations, and links to other science safety resources, is available at the Council of State Science Supervisors (CSSS) website at *www.csss-science. org/safety.shtml.* The National Science Teaching Association (NSTA) provides a list of science rules and regulations, including standard operating procedures for lab safety, and a safety acknowledgment form for students and parents or guardians to sign. You can access these resources at *http://static.nsta.org/pdfs/SafetyIn TheScienceClassroom.pdf.* In addition, NSTA's Safety in the Science Classroom web page (*www.nsta.org/safety*) has numerous links to safety resources, including papers written by the NSTA Safety Advisory Board.

Disclaimer: The safety precautions for each activity are based on use of the recommended materials and instructions, legal safety standards, and better professional practices. Using alternative materials or procedures for these activities may jeopardize the level of safety and therefore is at the user's own risk.

REFERENCES

Bandura, A. 1986. *Social foundations of thought and action: A social cognitive theory.* Englewood Cliffs, NJ: Prentice-Hall.

Barell, J. 2006. *Problem-based learning: An inquiry approach.* Thousand Oaks, CA: Corwin Press.

Benner, P. 1984. *From novice to expert: Excellence and power in clinical nursing practice.* Menlo Park, CA: Addison-Wesley Publishing Company.

Black, P., C. Harrison, C. Lee, B. Marshall, and D. Wiliam. 2003. *Assessment for learning: Putting it into practice.* Berkshire, UK: Open University Press.

Black, P., and D. Wiliam. 1998. Inside the black box: Raising standards through classroom assessment. *Phi Delta Kappan* 80 (2): 139–148.

Blumenfeld, P., E. Soloway, R. Marx, J. Krajcik, M. Guzdial, and A. Palincsar. 1991. Motivating project-based learning: Sustaining the doing, supporting learning. *Educational Psychologist* 26 (3): 369–398.

Brookhart, S. M., and A. J. Nitko. 2008. *Assessment and grading in classrooms.* Upper Saddle River, NJ: Pearson.

Bybee, R., J. Taylor, A. Gardner, P. Van Scotter, J. Carlson, A. Westbrook, and N. Landes. 2006. *The BSCS 5E instructional model: Origins and effectiveness. http://science.education.nih.gov/ houseofreps. nsf/b82d55fa138783c2852572c9004f5566/$FILE/Appendix?D.pdf.*

Eliason, C. F., and L. T. Jenkins. 2012. *A practical guide to early childhood curriculum.* 9th ed. New York: Merrill.

Johnson, C. 2003. Bioterrorism is real-world science: Inquiry-based simulation mirrors real life. *Science Scope* 27 (3): 19–23.

Krajcik, J., and P. Blumenfeld. 2006. Project-based learning. In *The Cambridge handbook of the learning sciences,* ed. R. Keith Sawyer, 317–334. New York: Cambridge University Press.

Lambros, A. 2004. *Problem-based learning in middle and high school classrooms: A teacher's guide to implementation.* Thousand Oaks, CA: Corwin Press.

Milner, A. R., and T. Sondergeld. 2015. Gifted urban middle school students: The inquiry continuum and the nature of science. *National Journal of Urban Education and Practice* 8 (3): 442–461.

Morrison, V., and A. R. Milner. 2014. Literacy in support of science: A closer look at cross-curricular instructional practice. *Michigan Reading Journal* 46 (2): 42–56.

National Association for the Education of Young Children (NAEYC). 2016. Developmentally appropriate practice position statements. *www.naeyc.org/positionstatements/dap.*

Peters, E. E. 2010. Shifting to a student-centered science classroom: An exploration of teacher and student changes in perceptions and practices. *Journal of Science Teacher Education* 21 (3): 329–349.

Peters, E. E. 2012. Developing content knowledge in students through explicit teaching of the nature of science: Influences of goal setting and self-monitoring. *Science and Education* 21 (6): 881–898.

Peters, E. E., and A. Kitsantas. 2010. The effect of nature of science metacognitive prompts on science students' content and nature of science knowledge, metacognition, and self-regulatory efficacy. *School Science and Mathematics* 110: 382–396.

Popham, W. J. 2013. *Classroom assessment: What teachers need to know.* 7th ed. Upper Saddle River, NJ: Pearson.

Ritchhart, R., M. Church, and K. Morrison. 2011. *Making thinking visible: How to promote engagement, understanding, and independence for all learners.* San Francisco, CA: Jossey-Bass.

Sondergeld, T. A., C. A. Bell, and D. M. Leusner. 2010. Understanding how teachers engage in formative assessment. *Teaching and Learning* 24 (2): 72–86.

Zimmerman, B. J. 2000. Attaining self-regulation: A social-cognitive perspective. In *Handbook of self-regulation,* ed. M. Boekaerts, P. Pintrich, and M. Zeidner, 13–39. San Diego: Academic Press.

PART 2

GENETICALLY MODIFIED ORGANISMS

STEM ROAD MAP MODULE

GENETICALLY MODIFIED ORGANISMS MODULE OVERVIEW

Stephen Burton, Janet B. Walton, Carla C. Johnson, and Erin E. Peters-Burton

THEME: Optimizing the Human Experience

LEAD DISCIPLINE: Social Studies and Science

MODULE SUMMARY

As America has moved farther from its rural roots, we have become less connected to the origin of the food we eat, so an understanding of our current food sources are necessary in order to make informed decisions about the food that we eat. Recent advances in molecular technology in the field of genetics is making significant strides in altering the genetic makeup of organisms, known as genetic engineering. Organisms that have been modified to turn on, off, or eliminate an organisms genes using the CRSPR technology show the promise for potential medical application for curing genetic diseases such as sickle cell anemia. Additionally, technology for inserting genes from bacteria providing resistance to herbicides or insect pests have been successfully inserted into plants. Since these organisms contain genes that are from two different species they are known as transgenic organisms.

The promise of genetic engineering is that it can much more quickly produce an organisms that can serve particular purposes than using traditional artificial selection and breeding that we have used to genetically modify organisms for centuries. In the 1990's, genetically engineered crops resistant to herbicides or insects were first introduced in the US agricultural market. Since its introduction, the reliance on crops that are genetically engineered through molecular technology has increased with 92% of all corn, 98% of all cotton, and 94% of all soybeans planted in the US in 2019 being genetically engineered.

With increased public awareness of the use of genetically engineered crops, there has also been increased concern about their safety within our food. Through popular media, the term genetically modified organism (GMO) has become synonymous

DOI: 10.4324/9781003261735-5

with genetically engineered organisms, especially transgenic organisms, even though humans have been genetically modifying organisms for centuries through artificial selection, grafting, etc. In this module, we will use the common usage of GMO that refers specifically to genetically engineered organisms. The idea of eating or interacting with a chimera has many in the public rightfully asking if this technology is safe. Additionally, groups are questioning the ethics of making transgenic organisms. Just because science has shown humans can do it, is it ethically appropriate for us to do it?

These technologies offer great promise for addressing challenges society currently faces, most namely disease and hunger, but this technology comes with concerns for both humans and the environment. Like many issues we face today, it is up to individuals to develop their own understanding of the issue.

Wading through rhetoric to determine the facts on which to make a decision can be challenging. For our students, the Internet is one of the primary ways in which they become more informed. As with other sources of information, students must make critical decisions about what Internet sources can be trusted. In this module, the students will be building the skills to become life-long learners and informed citizens by analyzing publicly available information about GMOs. This module engages students in a study of GMOs, focusing on the health, social, and economic implications of the increasing use of GMOs, reinforcing their ability to become life-long learners and informed citizens (adapted from Johnson et al., 2015; see https://www.routledge.com/products/9781138804234).

ESTABLISHED GOALS/OBJECTIVES

- Use the Internet and other sources to build knowledge of an issue (social studies and English language arts).

- Recognize and value stakeholders and their viewpoints in an issue (social studies and English language arts)

- Explore the relationship among local, state, and federal legislation related to GMOs (social studies).

- Understand the role of cost-benefit analysis in making informed economic decisions (mathematics and social studies)

- Develop skills to evaluate arguments, create and communicate individual understanding and perspectives (English language arts).

- Gain a deeper understanding that structure and function are related by examining plants and how the environment and genetics influences structure (science).

- Gain a better understanding of what tools humans have developed to genetically alter organisms for human benefit (science and social studies).

CHALLENGE AND/OR PROBLEM FOR STUDENTS TO SOLVE

GMO Documentary

Students will create a documentary communicating the health, social, and economic aspects of GMO production and consumption. Each class will create its own documentary in segments focusing on different aspects of the GMO issue. Over the course of the module, all students will develop knowledge regarding the concepts related to all of these segments, however, student groups will be assigned as the lead creators of different segments when they begin the documentary production.

- Introduction – 5 min – Created by the teacher with assistance from the kids.

- Segment 1–10 min

  o What is a GMO? How are they created?
  o What are examples of GMOs that currently exist?
  o How have organisms' genetic makeups been altered in the past?

- Segment 2–10 min

  o What are possible benefits from GMOs in agriculture?

- Segment 3–10 min

  o What are possible threats from GMOs in agriculture?

- Segment 4–10 min

  o Who are the stakeholders and what are their stances?

- Segment 5–10 min

  o What is the government at the local, state, and federal levels doing to address the concerns of stakeholders?

CONTENT STANDARDS ADDRESSED IN THIS STEM ROAD MAP MODULE

A full listing with descriptions of the standards this module addresses can be found in the appendix. Listings of the particular standards addressed within lessons are provided in a table for each lesson in Chapter 4.

STEM RESEARCH NOTEBOOK

Each student should maintain a STEM Research Notebook, which will serve as a place for students to organize their work throughout this module (see p. 12 for more general discussion on setup and use of the notebook). All written work in the module should be included in the notebook, including records of students' thoughts and ideas, fictional accounts based on the concepts in the module, and records of student progress through the EDP. The notebooks may be maintained across subject areas, giving students the opportunity to see that although their classes may be separated during the school day, the knowledge they gain is connected. You may also wish to have students include the STEM Research Notebook Guidelines student handout on page 29 in their notebooks.

Emphasize to students the importance of organizing all information in a Research Notebook. Explain to them that scientists and other researchers maintain detailed Research Notebooks in their work. These notebooks, which are crucial to researchers' work because they contain critical information and track the researchers' progress, are often considered legal documents for scientists who are pursuing patents or wish to provide proof of their discovery process.

STEM RESEARCH NOTEBOOK GUIDELINES

STEM professionals record their ideas, inventions, experiments, questions, observations, and other work details in notebooks so that they can use these notebooks to help them think about their projects and the problems they are trying to solve. You will each keep a STEM Research Notebook during this module that is like the notebooks that STEM professionals use. In this notebook, you will include all your work and notes about ideas you have. The notebook will help you connect your daily work with the big problem or challenge you are working to solve.

It is important that you organize your notebook entries under the following headings:

1. **Chapter Topic or Title of Problem or Challenge:** You will start a new chapter in your STEM Research Notebook for each new module. This heading is the topic or title of the big problem or challenge that your team is working to solve in this module.

2. **Date and Topic of Lesson Activity for the Day:** Each day, you will begin your daily entry by writing the date and the day's lesson topic at the top of a new page. Write the page number both on the page and in the table of contents.

3. **Information Gathered from Research:** This is information you find from outside resources such as websites or books.

4. **Information Gained from Class or Discussions with Team Members:** This information includes any notes you take in class and notes about things your team discusses. You can include drawings of your ideas here, too.

5. **New Data Collected from Investigations:** This includes data gathered from experiments, investigations, and activities in class.

6. **Documents:** These are handouts and other resources you may receive in class that will help you solve your big problem or challenge. Paste or staple these documents in your STEM Research Notebook for safekeeping and easy access later.

7. **Personal Reflections:** Here, you record your own thoughts and ideas on what you are learning.

8. **Lesson Prompts:** These are questions or statements that your teacher assigns you within each lesson to help you solve your big problem or challenge. You will respond to the prompts in your notebook.

9. **Other Items:** This section includes any other items your teacher gives you or other ideas or questions you may have.

MODULE LAUNCH

Launch the module in social studies by leading a discussion regarding the type of food kids like to eat, focusing students on types of fruits and vegetables in particular. Emphasize that many of the fruits and vegetables we find in the supermarket are not normally found in the wild, but have been generated in a variety of ways dating to ancient times, when humans began domesticating wild plants (the beginning of agriculture). Explain that we continue to alter plants in a variety of ways, but in the past 20 years, a new method has emerged. Introduce the concept of GMOs and genetically engineered (GE) organisms and show a video describing the GMO issue generally. Tell the students that they will be challenged to create a documentary that will help citizens become better informed about the health, social, and economic aspects of GMO production and consumption.

PREREQUISITE SKILLS FOR THE MODULE

Students enter this module with a wide range of preexisting skills, information, and knowledge. Table 3.1 provides an overview of prerequisite skills and knowledge

Table 3.1. Prerequisite Key Knowledge and Examples of Applications and Differentiation Strategies

Prerequisite key knowledge	Application of knowledge	Differentiation for students needing knowledge
Science		
• The role that DNA and genes play in producing traits	• Examining different fast-plants produced through selective breeding	• Use on-line simulations to demonstrate that DNA produces genes which produce a trait
Mathematics		
• Ability to use calculation tools such as graphing calculators or computer spreadsheets	• Creating the cost-benefit analysis and generating graphs and descriptive statistics	• Spend time in class assisting students with skills during the activity
English language arts		
• Conduct Internet searches using key words • Ability to read non-fiction writing	• Students will use the Internet and other non-fiction sources for generating their information gathering for the GMO documentary	• Assist students with Internet searches during the activity • Have available a variety of resources that could be used by students at different reading levels • Group students with varying abilities in reading to conduct the Internet searches

that students are expected to apply in this module, along with examples of how they apply this knowledge throughout the module. Differentiation strategies are also provided for students who may need additional support in acquiring or applying this knowledge.

POTENTIAL STEM MISCONCEPTIONS

Students enter the classroom with a wide variety of prior knowledge and ideas, so it is important to be alert to misconceptions, or inappropriate understandings of foundational knowledge. These misconceptions can be classified as one of several types: "preconceived notions," opinions based on popular beliefs or understandings; "nonscientific beliefs," knowledge students have gained about science from sources outside the scientific community; "conceptual misunderstandings," incorrect conceptual models based on incomplete understanding of concepts; "vernacular misconceptions," misunderstandings of words based on their common use versus their scientific use; and "factual misconceptions," incorrect or imprecise knowledge learned in early life that remains unchallenged (NRC 1997, p. 28). Misconceptions must be addressed and dismantled in order for students to reconstruct their knowledge, and therefore teachers should be prepared to take the following steps:

- *Identify students' misconceptions.*

- *Provide a forum for students to confront their misconceptions.*

- *Help students reconstruct and internalize their knowledge, based on scientific models. (NRC 1997, p. 29)*

Keeley and Harrington (2010) recommend using diagnostic tools such as probes and formative assessment to identify and confront student misconceptions and begin the process of reconstructing student knowledge. Keeley and Harrington's *Uncovering Student Ideas in Science* series contains probes targeted toward uncovering student misconceptions in a variety of areas.

Some commonly held misconceptions specific to lesson content are provided with each lesson so that you can be alert for student misunderstanding of the science

Table 3.2. Sample STEM Misconceptions

Topic	Student Misconception	Explanation
Data communication	Any graph can be used to display data	The research question and type of data will limit the type of graphs that can be used to communicate data
Genes	Genes are the only determinant of your expressed characteristics	Although genes play an important role and provide the framework in which you characteristics can be expressed, environment also influence expression of your characteristics

concepts presented and used during this module. The American Association for the Advancement of Science has also identified misconceptions that students frequently hold regarding various science concepts (see the links at *http://assessment.aaas.org/topics*).

Table 3.3 illustrates some of the activities in the GMO module and how they align to the SRL process before, during, and after learning.

Table 3.3. SRL Learning Process Components

Learning Process Components	Example from GMOs Module	Lesson in module
Before Learning		
Motivates students	Students watch a video describing GMOs and think about the origins of their own food sources.	Lesson 1
Evokes prior learning	Students tap into their prior experience with GMOs/GE and relate it to what they already know about food production and consumption.	Lesson 1
During Learning		
Focuses on important features	Students use a graphic organizer to help them compile all of the necessary components of an argument for the pros and cons of GMO uses.	Lesson 2
Helps students monitor their progress	Students are provided feedback for their class participation during the arguments and for the selection of appropriate resources to develop their argument.	Lesson 2
After Learning		
Evaluates learning	In the final challenge, students create a documentary communicating the health, social, and economic aspects of GMO production and consumption. Students do an initial review before presenting to parents and friends.	Lesson 5
Takes account of what worked and what did not work	In the final challenge, students reflect on the initial review and reactions from parents and friends to their documentary video.	Lesson 5

STRATEGIES FOR DIFFERENTIATING INSTRUCTION WITHIN THIS MODULE

For the purposes of this curriculum module, differentiated instruction is conceptualized as a way to tailor instruction—including process, content, and product—to various student needs in your class. A number of differentiation strategies are integrated into lessons across the module. The problem- and project-based learning approach used in the lessons is designed to address students' multiple intelligences by providing a variety of entry points and methods to investigate the key concepts in the module (for example, investigating gardening from the perspectives of science and social issues via scientific inquiry, literature, journaling, and collaborative design). Differentiation strategies for students needing support in prerequisite knowledge can be found in Table 3.1 (p. 30). You are encouraged to use information gained about student prior knowledge during introductory activities and discussions to inform your instructional differentiation. Strategies incorporated into this lesson include flexible grouping, varied environmental learning contexts, assessments, compacting, tiered assignments, and scaffolding.

Flexible Grouping: Students have the opportunity to learn in various contexts throughout the module, including alone, in groups, in quiet reading and research-oriented activities, and in active learning through inquiry and design activities. In addition, students learn in a variety of ways, including through doing inquiry activities, journaling, reading texts, watching videos, participating in class discussion, and conducting web-based research.

Varied Environmental Learning Contexts: Students have the opportunity to learn in various contexts throughout the module, including alone, in groups, in quiet reading and research-oriented activities, and in active learning through inquiry and design activities. In addition, students learn in a variety of ways, including through doing inquiry activities, journaling, reading a variety of texts, watching videos, participating in class discussion, and conducting web-based research.

Assessments: Students are assessed in a variety of ways throughout the module, including individual and collaborative formative and summative assessments. Students have the opportunity to produce work via written text, oral and media presentations, and modeling. You may choose to provide students with additional choices of media for their products (for example, PowerPoint presentations, posters, or student-created websites or blogs).

Compacting: Based on student prior knowledge, you may wish to adjust instructional activities for students who exhibit prior mastery of a learning objective. You may wish to compile a classroom database of research resources and supplementary readings for a variety of reading levels and on a variety of topics related to the module's topic to provide opportunities for students to undertake independent reading.

Tiered Assignments and Scaffolding: Based on your awareness of student ability, understanding of concepts, and mastery of skills, you may wish to provide students with variations on activities by adding complexity to assignments or providing more or fewer learning supports for activities throughout the module. For instance, some students may need additional support in identifying key search words and phrases for web-based research or may benefit from cloze sentence handouts to enhance vocabulary understanding. Other students may benefit from expanded reading selections and additional reflective writing or from working with manipulatives and other visual representations of mathematical concepts. You may also work with your school librarian to compile a set of topical resources at a variety of reading levels.

STRATEGIES FOR ENGLISH LANGUAGE LEARNERS

Students who are developing proficiency in English language skills require additional supports to simultaneously learn academic content and the specialized language associated with specific content areas. WIDA has created a framework for providing support to these students and makes available rubrics and guidance on differentiating instructional materials for English language learners (ELLs) (see *www.wida.us/get.aspx?id=7*). In particular, ELL students may benefit from additional sensory supports such as images, physical modeling, and graphic representations of module content, as well as interactive support through collaborative work. This module incorporates a variety of sensory supports and provides ongoing opportunities for ELL students to work collaboratively.

Teachers differentiating instruction for ELL students should carefully consider the needs of these students as they introduce and use academic language in various language domains (listening, speaking, reading, and writing) throughout this module. To adequately differentiate instruction for ELL students, teachers should have an understanding of the proficiency level of each student. The following five overarching 9–12 WIDA learning standards are relevant to this module:

Standard 1: Social and instructional language. Focus on social behavior in group work and class discussions.

Standard 2: The language of language arts. Focus on forms of print, elements of text, picture books, comprehension strategies, main ideas and details, persuasive language, creating informational text, and editing and revising.

Standard 3: The language of mathematics. Focus on numbers and operations, patterns, number sense, measurement, and strategies for problem solving.

Standard 4: The language of science. Focus on safety practices, energy sources, scientific process, and scientific inquiry.

Standard 5: The language of social studies. Focus on change from past to present, historical events, resources, transportation, map reading, and location of objects and places.

SAFETY CONSIDERATIONS FOR THE ACTIVITIES IN THIS MODULE

There are no major concerns regarding safety during this module. In Science, students will be working with plants including using forceps and probes to dissect seeds. Additionally, they will be using microscopes and glass slides. Focusing on good hygiene and no horseplay during investigations will reduce safety concerns. In English language arts and social studies, students will be accessing information using the internet. Care should be taken to protect students from accessing internet sites that are inappropriate. Your IT contact person can provide guidance for appropriate search engines. Additionally, they may already have protective measures in place to prevent the students from accessing inappropriate content. For more precautions, see the specific safety notes after the list of materials in each lesson. For more general safety guidelines, see the Safety in STEM section in Chapter 2 (p. 19).

DESIRED OUTCOMES AND MONITORING SUCCESS

The desired outcomes for this module are outlined in Table 3.4, along with suggested ways to gather evidence to monitor student success. For more specific details on desired outcomes, see the Established Goals and Objectives sections for the module and individual lessons.

Table 3.4. Desired Outcomes and Evidence of Success in Achieving Identified Outcomes

Desired Outcome	Evidence of Success in Achieving Identified Outcome	
	Performance Tasks	Other Measures
Students will create a documentary communicating the health, social, and economic aspects of GMO production and consumption.	• Students will maintain STEM Research Notebooks that will contain designs, research notes, evidence of collaboration, and English language arts-related work • **Students will be assessed on whether their documentary illustrates an understanding of** GMOs; stakeholders associated with the GMO issue and their viewpoints; benefits and threats of GMOs with accurate scientific and societal understanding; the role of local, state, and federal governments in regulating GMOs.	**Students' collaboration on the documentary, participation in classroom discussions, and specific tasks related to finding relevant and reliable information as well as using the information appropriately in communication.**

ASSESSMENT PLAN OVERVIEW AND MAP

Table 3.5 provides an overview of the major group and individual *products* and *deliverables*, or things that student teams will produce in this module, that constitute the assessment for this module. See Table 3.6 for a full assessment map of formative and summative assessments in this module.

Table 3.5. Major Products and Deliverables in Lead Disciplines for Groups and Individuals

Lesson	Major Group Products/Deliverables	Major Individual Products/Deliverables
1	• none	• Appropriate resource selection assignment • Summarized learning assignment • STEM Research Notebook prompt
2	• none	• Argument Graphic Organizer • Cost-benefit analysis • STEM Research Notebook prompt
3	• Recommendations to farmers	• Data communication of investigations • STEM Research Notebook prompt
4	• Initial organization that includes important facts and how they will start and end their documentary • Interview Questions	• STEM Research Notebook prompt
5	• Storyboard	• none

Table 3.6. Assessment Chart, Lead Disciplines – Genetically Modified Organisms

Lesson	Assessment	Group/Individual	Formative/Summative	Lesson Objective Assessed (students will:)
1	Resource Selection assignment	Group	Formative	Determine the information necessary to become well informed regarding an issue. Describe effective ways to use technology and the Internet to find information regarding an issue.
1	GMO Summary assignment	Group	Formative	Describe the stakeholders associated with an issue.

Continued

Table 3.6. (*Continued*)

Lesson	Assessment	Group/ Individual	Formative/ Summative	Lesson Objective Assessed (students will:)
1	STEM Research Notebook - lab entries	Individual	Formative	Explain the function of the root, stem and leaf of a plant Describe the development of an embryonic plant during germination Define tissue Describe the role of the meristematic tissue, epidermal tissue, and vascular tissue in the root.
1	STEM Research Notebook prompts (webquest)	Individual	Formative	Determine the information necessary to become well informed regarding an issue. Describe the stakeholders associated with an issue. Describe effective ways to use technology and the Internet to find information regarding an issue.
2	Argument graphic organizer	Individual	Formative	Describe how the viewpoint of an individual will influence what arguments are compelling. Describe ways to compromise such that all stakeholders' viewpoints are considered.
2	Cost-Benefit Analysis	Group	Formative	Use cost-benefit analysis as a way to evaluate pros and cons of an issue.
2	STEM Research Notebook - lab entries	Individual	Summative	Explain the function of the root, stem and leaf of a plant. Describe the role of the meristematic tissue, epidermal tissue, and vascular tissue in the stem and leaves. Describe the anatomical features that allow leaves to perform photosynthesis.

Continued

Table 3.6. (*Continued*)

Lesson	Assessment	Group/ Individual	Formative/ Summative	Lesson Objective Assessed (students will:)
2	STEM Research Notebook prompts (webquest)	Individual	Summative	Explain the function of the root, stem and leaf of a plant. Describe the role of the meristematic tissue, epidermal tissue, and vascular tissue in the stem and leaves. Describe the anatomical features that allow leaves to perform photosynthesis.
3	Data Communication activity	Individual	Formative	Students will be able to describe the role of descriptive statistics in summarizing data for communication and analysis.
3	Farmer Recommendations	Group	Formative	Students will be able to describe how the environment influences the growth and development of organisms.
3	STEM Research Notebook - lab entries	Individual	Summative	Students will be able to describe how the environment influences the growth and development of organisms.
3	STEM Research Notebook prompts (webquest)	Individual	Formative	Students will be able to define plagiarism, paraphrasing, and quoting. Students will be able to create examples of plagiarism, paraphrasing, and the use of quotations. Students will explain why plagiarism is not appropriate. Students will explain how to paraphrase and use quotations effectively in a communication.

Continued

Table 3.6. (*Continued*)

Lesson	Assessment	Group/ Individual	Formative/ Summative	Lesson Objective Assessed (students will:)
4	Presentation - Structure and Content of Documentaries	Group	Formative	Students will be able to explain how information literacy has changed in the past 40 years. Students will describe how they will engage their viewers as well as close their section in a way that makes their documentary contribution a unified whole.
4	STEM Research Notebook - lab entries	Individual	Formative	Students will be able to explain how variations in a gene can result in different traits in an organism. Students will be able to describe how humans have influenced the inheritance of desired traits in organisms through selective breeding.
4	STEM Research Notebook prompts (webquest)	Individual	Formative	Students will be able to explain how variations in a gene can result in different traits in an organism. Students will be able to describe how humans have influenced the inheritance of desired traits in organisms through selective breeding.
5	Documentary presentation	Group	Summative	Students will be able to use storyboarding to organize their documentary for both shooting video, writing script, and editing. Students will demonstrate their scientific understanding of GMOs and the societal issues surrounding the use of GMOs.
5	Evidence of collaboration	Individual	Summative	Students will demonstrate their ability to collaborate with peers to organize information and create a product.

MODULE TIMELINE

Tables 3.7–3.11 (pp. 40–42) provide lesson timelines for each week of the module. These timelines are provided for general guidance only and are based on class times of approximately 45 minutes.

STEM Road Map Module Timeline

Table 3.7. STEM Road Map Module Schedule Week One

Day 1	Day 2	Day 3	Day 4	Day 5
Lesson 1	*Lesson 1*	*Lesson 1*	*Lesson 1*	*Lesson 1*
WHAT ARE GMO's AND WHY ARE THEY IN THE NEWS?	WHAT ARE GMO's AND WHY ARE THEY IN THE NEWS?	WHAT ARE GMO's AND WHY ARE THEY IN THE NEWS?	WHAT ARE GMO's AND WHY ARE THEY IN THE NEWS?	WHAT ARE GMO's AND WHY ARE THEY IN THE NEWS?
Launch the module by watching video describing GMOs in general then discuss strategies for gathering information. Start plants and discuss what students already know about plants.	Explore ways to identify relevant and reliable resources, continue finding resources to determine what a GMO is and who might be impacted by GMOs, conduct a webquest for understanding seeds and roots.	Explore ways to take notes on resources, continue finding resources to determine what a GMO is and who might be impacted by GMOs, continue webquest for understanding seeds and roots.	Continue finding resources to determine what a GMO is and who might be impacted by GMOs and begin writing two page summary, continue webquest for understanding seeds and roots.	Discuss finding from GMO search and seeds and roots webquest.

Table 3.8. STEM Road Map Module Schedule Week Two

Day 6	Day 7	Day 8	Day 9	Day 10
Lesson 2	*Lesson 2*	*Lesson 2*	*Lesson 2*	*Lesson 2*
HOW DO WE MAKE DECISIONS ABOUT GMOS?	HOW DO WE MAKE DECISIONS ABOUT GMOS?	HOW DO WE MAKE DECISIONS ABOUT GMOS?	HOW DO WE MAKE DECISIONS ABOUT GMOS?	HOW DO WE MAKE DECISIONS ABOUT GMOS?
Explore the pros and cons of GMOs, start cost-benefit analysis, begin understanding arguments, begin exploration of stems and leaves.	Continue exploring the pros and cons of GMOs, continue cost-benefit analysis, continue developing understanding of arguments, exploration of stems and leaves.	Continue exploring the pros and cons of GMOs, continue cost-benefit analysis, use argumentation graphic organizer, exploration of stems and leaves.	Examine cost-benefit analysis regarding GMO, examine stakeholder viewpoint determining compelling arguments, continue exploration of stems and leaves.	Develop a compromise on GMO balancing all viewpoints, write a compelling argument, discuss findings of stem and leaf webquest, propose how environment might alter growth.

Table 3.9. STEM Road Map Module Schedule Week Three

Day 11	Day 12	Day 13	Day 14	Day 15
Lesson 3	*Lesson 3*	*Lesson 3*	*Lesson 3*	*Lesson 3*
WHAT ROLE SHOULD THE GOVERNMENT PLAY IN GMOS?	WHAT ROLE SHOULD THE GOVERNMENT PLAY IN GMOS?	WHAT ROLE SHOULD THE GOVERNMENT PLAY IN GMOS?	WHAT ROLE SHOULD THE GOVERNMENT PLAY IN GMOS?	WHAT ROLE SHOULD THE GOVERNMENT PLAY IN GMOS?
Examine government involvement in GMO issue, explore plagiarism/paraphrasing/ quoting, measure plants, investigate and interpret graphs and descriptive statistics.	Examine government involvement in GMO issue, explore plagiarism/ paraphrasing/quoting, investigate and interpret graphs and descriptive statistics and apply to plant data.	Examine government involvement in GMO issue, organizing and writing communication for GMO, investigate and interpret graphs and descriptive statistics and apply to plant data.	Examine government involvement in GMO issue, organizing and writing communication about GMOs, use data communications to develop argument for impact of fertilizer levels on plant growth.	Discuss government involvement in GMO issue, organizing and writing communication about GMOs, use data communications to develop argument for impact of fertilizer levels on plant growth.

Table 3.10. STEM Road Map Module Schedule Week Four

Day 16	Day 17	Day 18	Day 19	Day 20
Lesson 4	*Lesson 4*	*Lesson 4*	*Lesson 4*	*Lesson 4*
DOES THE MEDIA INFLUENCE OUR PERSPECTIVES?	DOES THE MEDIA INFLUENCE OUR PERSPECTIVES?	DOES THE MEDIA INFLUENCE OUR PERSPECTIVES?	DOES THE MEDIA INFLUENCE OUR PERSPECTIVES?	DOES THE MEDIA INFLUENCE OUR PERSPECTIVES?
Explore how others get information without the Internet, organize structure and information for documentary, examine impact of genes on plants.	Present findings on how others get information without the Internet, present organizational ideas to class, investigate impacts of radiation on plants.	Investigate balanced reporting in resources, plan interviews, exploring methods used to generate GMOs.	Discuss different societal responses to GMO and selective breeding, conduct interviews, investigate selective breeding impacts on genetic makeup of plants.	Conduct interviews, share findings on selective breeding impacts on genetic makeup of plants.

Table 3.11. STEM Road Map Module Schedule Week Five

Day 21	Day 22	Day 23	Day 24	Day 25
Lesson 5	*Lesson 5*	*Lesson 5*	*Lesson 5*	*Lesson 5*
PUTTING IT ALL TOGETHER	PUTTING IT ALL TOGETHER	PUTTING IT ALL TOGETHER	PUTTING IT ALL TOGETHER	PUTTING IT ALL TOGETHER
Students storyboard their documentary segments.	Present ideas to peers and teachers, video record, edit videos.	Present ideas to peers and teachers, video record, edit videos.	Final day of editing, complete video.	Present final videos to peers, premier to parents and friends.

RESOURCES

Teachers have the option to co-teach portions of this module and may want to combine classes for activities. Computer science teachers can help students develop graphic images or animations, and art teachers can help students create three-dimensional models. The media specialist can help teachers locate resources for students to view and read about genetically modified organism production and issues surrounding the need to meet society's food needs. Special educators and reading specialists can help find supplemental sources for students needing extra support in reading and writing. Additional resources may be found online. Community resources for this module may include guest speakers who work in GMO production and farming, and those involved in resource conservation efforts related to food production and preparation.

REFERENCES

Keeley, P. and R. Harrington. 2010. *Uncovering student ideas in physical science, volume 1: 45 new force and motion assessment probes.* Arlington, VA: NSTA Press.

National Center for O*NET Development. *Find Occupations.* Retrieved from https://www. onetonline.org/find/

Peters-Burton, E. E., P. Seshaiyer, S. R. Burton, J. Drake-Patrick, and C. C. Johnson. 2015. The STEM Road Map for grades 9–12. In *STEM Road Map: A framework for integrated STEM education*, ed. C. C. Johnson, E. E. Peters-Burton, and T. J. Moore, 124–62. New York: Routledge. *www.routledge.com/products/9781138804234.*

WIDA Consortium. 2012. 2012 Amplification of the English language development standards: Kindergarten – grade 12. *www.wida.us/standards/eld.aspx.*

GENETICALLY MODIFIED ORGANISMS MODULE LESSON PLANS

Stephen Burton, Janet B. Walton, Carla C. Johnson, and Erin E. Peters-Burton

Lesson Plan 1: What Are GMO's and Why Are They in the News?

LESSON SUMMARY

In social studies, students will be introduced to their challenge and work to figure out the most important questions to answer to develop knowledge regarding genetically modified organisms (GMOs). Students will focus on gathering resources and formulating a summary of the issue.

In English language arts, students will be using teacher resources to identify relevant and reliable resources and summarizing information from the resources. They will also apply this knowledge to their own review of resources related to GMOs.

Since most GMOs in agriculture are plants, students will investigate plants to understand how the environment and genes influence organisms. In particular, they will be exploring developing seeds to determine structure and function, focusing on the organization of cells into tissues, tissues into organs, and organs into the functioning plant. This lesson will focus on root development, structure, and function.

ESSENTIAL QUESTION(S)

Science

- What are the parts of a plant and how do they help it survive?

- What happens to a seed after it has been planted?

- What is the role of the roots and how do plants grow?

DOI: 10.4324/9781003261735-6

Mathematics

N/A

English Language Arts

- How can we determine what resources are relevant and reliable?

- How can we figure out what in a reading will be relevant and useful in developing knowledge of a topic?

Social Studies

- Why should we care about GMOs?

- What are good questions to ask to understand the GMO issue?

ESTABLISHED GOALS/OBJECTIVES
Science

- Explain the function of the root, stem and leaf of a plant

- Describe the development of an embryonic plant during germination

- Define tissue

- Describe the role of the meristematic tissue, epidermal tissue, and vascular tissue in the root.

Mathematics

N/A

English Language Arts

- Describe what makes a resource reliable and relevant in learning about a topic.

- Identify the relevant and useful content within a reading.

- Describe effective ways of documenting knowledge development within and among difference sources

Social Studies

- Determine the information necessary to become well informed regarding an issue.

- Describe the stakeholders associated with an issue

- Describe effective ways to use technology and the Internet to find information regarding an issue.

TIME REQUIRED – 5 DAYS (45-MINUTE CLASS PERIODS)
NECESSARY MATERIALS
Science

- Day 1

  o Wisconsin Fast Plants ® Exploring Variation Kit – http://www.carolina.com/wfp-plant-growth-and-development/exploring-variation-with-wisconsin-fast-plants-kit/158706.pr?question=

  o Wisconsin Fast Plants ® Irradiated Seed Kit – http://www.carolina.com/wfp-genetics/wisconsin-fast-plants-irradiated-seed-kit/FAM_158750.pr?question=

  o Wisconsin Fast Plants ® Nutrition Study Kit – http://www.carolina.com/wfp-environmental-science/wisconsin-fast-plants-nutrition-study-kit/FAM_158720.pr?question=#family-details

- Days 2–4

  o Germinating seeds at different stages (bean seeds should be soaked overnight and placed on wet paper towels on trays starting one week before the lesson and adding a new batch of seeds each day until the day of the lesson).

  o Microscopes (dissecting and compound).

  o Prepared microscope slides – root cells showing both the meristematic tissue as well as areas of elongation, root cross section showing different cell types.

- Day 5

  o Computers with Internet access for groups of students. Optional: list of starting sites or key words for students.

English Language Arts

- Day 1

  N/A

- Day 2

  o Computers with Internet access for groups of students.

  o Example resources for examining an issue associated with GMOs – these should include reliable and non-reliable sources as well as examples that are tangential to the overall questions. There should be multiple examples on which students will build their understanding of how to determine reliability and relevance.

  o Students should bring the resources they identified in social studies.

- Day 3

    o   Computers with Internet access for groups of students.
    o   2–3 example resources that have been determined to be relevant and reliable for the GMO issue. These resources will be what students will use to determine how to identify the most important information in the reading.
    o   Students should bring the resources they identified in social studies.

- Days 4–5

    o   Computers with Internet access for groups of students.

Social Studies

- Days 1–5

    o   Computers with Internet access for groups of students.

Table 4.1. Content Standards Addressed in STEM Road Map Module Lesson One

---

NEXT GENERATION SCIENCE STANDARDS

PERFORMANCE OBJECTIVES
MS-LS1–3 – Use argument supported by evidence for how the body is a system of interacting subsystems composed of groups of cells.

Disciplinary Core Ideas and Crosscutting Concepts
LS1.A: Structure and Function – In multicellular organisms, the body is a system of multiple interacting subsystems. These subsystems are groups of cells that work together to form tissues and organs that are specialized for particular body functions (MS-LS1-3)
LS1.B: Growth and Development of Organisms – Organisms reproduce, either sexually or asexually, and transfer their genetic information to their offspring (secondary to MSLS3-2)

Science and Engineering Practices
CONSTRUCTING EXPLANATIONS AND DESIGNING SOLUTIONS – Constructing explanations and designing solutions in 6–8 builds on K–5 experiences and progresses to include constructing explanations and designing solutions supported by multiple sources of evidence consistent with scientific ideas, principles, and theories. Apply scientific ideas to construct an explanation for realworld phenomena, examples, or events. (MS-LS4–2); Construct an explanation that includes qualitative or quantitative relationships between variables that describe phenomena (MS-LS4–4)
OBTAINING, EVALUATING, AND COMMUNICATING INFORMATION – Obtaining, evaluating, and communicating information in 6–8 builds on K–5 experiences and progresses to evaluating the merit and validity of ideas and methods. Gather, read, and synthesize information from multiple appropriate sources and assess the credibility, accuracy, and possible bias of each publication and methods used, and describe how they are supported or not supported by evidence (MS-LS4–5)

Continued

Table 4.1 (*continued*)

> *COMMON CORE MATHEMATICS STANDARDS*
> N/A
>
> *COMMON CORE ENGLISH LANGUAGE ARTS*
>
> WRITING STANDARDS
> CCSS. English Language Arts-LITERACY.W.7.1.A – Introduce claim(s), acknowledge alternate or opposing claims, and organize the reasons and evidence logically.
> W.7.1.B – Support claim(s) with logical reasoning and relevant evidence, using accurate, credible sources and demonstrating an understanding of the topic or text.
> W.7.1.C – Use words, phrases, and clauses to create cohesion and clarify the relationships among claim(s), reasons, and evidence.
> W.7.1.E – Provide a concluding statement or section that follows from and supports the argument presented.
>
> *Reading Standards*
> RI.7.8 – Trace and evaluate the argument and specific claims in a text, assessing whether the reasoning is sound and the evidence is relevant and sufficient to support the claims.
> RI.7.9 – Analyze how two or more authors writing about the same topic shape their presentations of key information by emphasizing different evidence or advancing different interpretations of facts.
>
> *21st Century Skills (www.p21.org)*
> Environmental Literacy, Critical Thinking and Problem Solving, Information Literacy

Table 4.2. Key Vocabulary in Lesson One

Key Vocabulary	Definition
Cotyledon	Often called seed leaves – these specialized leaves transfer the nutrients from seed to embryonic plant. The nutrients found in the leaves were provided by the mother plant.
Gene	Specific sequence of DNA that codes for a particular trait.
Genetically modified organism (GMO)	Any organism whose genetic material has been altered using genetic engineering techniques – also known as transgenic.
Genome	The complete genetic makeup of an organism. This genetic makeup is in the form of DNA and contains the instructions for the function of each living cell in the organism.
Meristem	Region of specialized cells (tissues) within the plant that produces new cells through mitosis. Meristematic tissue is often found at the tips of the plant but can also be found to form in places where there is secondary growth or repair to the plant is needed.

Continued

Table 4.2. (*continued*)

Key Vocabulary	Definition
Mitosis	Process of cell division in which two new cells are formed from a parent cell.
Root	Section of plant (could be considered analogous to an organ in humans) that typically functions to obtain moisture from the environment and provide it for plant function; roots also serve the function of providing stability for plants to grow upward toward light.
Shoot/Stem	Section of the plant (could be considered analogous to an organ in humans) that provides structural support for the leaves and moves water from the roots up, allowing photosynthesis to occur in the leaves.
Stakeholders	Individuals with an interest or concern in an issue. These are individuals that are impacted (negatively or positively, directly or indirectly) by the issue and therefore may have a particular stance or perspective.
Tissue	A group of similar cells that perform a similar function.
Trait	A genetically determined characteristic

* Vocabulary terms are provided for both teacher and student use. Teachers may
choose to introduce all or some terms to students.

TEACHER BACKGROUND INFORMATION
Science

In lesson 1, students will explore developing seeds to examine seed germination, general plant anatomy, specific root anatomy and function, and plant tissues associated with root function. Students will make observations and gather evidence to propose what is happening to the seeds between the time they were planted and when the sprouts first appear. Students will maintain STEM research notebooks that describe their investigations, their observations, and answers to questions explored in webquests. More information regarding the use of lab notebooks can be found at – http:// www.plantingscience.org/index.php?module=content&func=view&pid=117.

At the end of the week, students should be able to explain the plant structures they see and relate them to their general functions (roots bringing in water and providing support for plant; stems providing support for leaves and transit between root and leaves; leaves as the site of photosynthesis). In their observations students should describe how the roots are growing (i.e., by producing new cells (at the root tip) and elongating them, allowing the root to stretch). They should be able to relate that the root provides support as well obtaining water and nutrients from the soil. Likewise, the root hairs they observe are useful in anchoring the root but also helps get more water from the soil. Students should also gain an understanding that areas of cells that function for a particular purpose are called tissue. The cells in the root make up the epidermal tissue that protects the root as it pushes through the soil, the vascular tissue that moves water and nutrients to and from the roots, and the meristematic tissue where cell division is the primary function. Students should also recognize that all of these tissues work together to set up the new plant so it can grow upward toward light and perform photosynthesis.

Mathematics

N/A

English Language Arts

Identifying relevant information within a text is critical in working to synthesize appropriate knowledge. This can be done in several ways; resources to support students with these techniques can be found at the following websites:

- http://www.skillsyouneed.com/write/notes-reading.html

- http://www.scholastic.com/teachers/article/grades-6-8-activities-teach-note-taking

- http://www.educationworld.com/a_lesson/lesson/lesson322.shtml

Social Studies

Humans have been working to modify the genetic makeup of organisms to benefit us for millennia, beginning with the domestication of organisms for agricultural purposes. Domestication and breeding for specific traits was accomplished through selective breeding. This method requires that organisms with a desired trait (or some of the desired trait) are bred together so that the trait of interest is either maintained or expressed to a greater extent. Selective breeding uses the natural reproductive process, but involves making intentional decisions about what individuals are passing on their genes. This is a slow and methodical process, requiring enough variation in the trait among offspring that another cross can be made with another in which the trait is even more magnified. This process of altering the genetic makeup through artificial selection and breeding has produced the majority of the plants and animals used in agriculture and foods. Unfortunately, however, it is a slow, painstaking process.

New technology arose with the increasing understanding of the role of DNA in organisms' genes and the expression of these genes in individual traits. Understanding how DNA is replicated and how genes produce traits has allowed biologists to figure out how to alter organisms DNA in the lab rather than waiting out the natural breeding process. The DNA of all living organisms are made up of the same four nucleotides, making it possible to transfer a gene found in a completely different species into a target organism, potentially resulting in the target organism expressing this new gene. When an organism's genetic makeup is altered in the lab to include genes from a different species, they are considered a genetically modified organism (GMO) but more specifically a transgenic organism. Desirable traits such as the ability to produce natural chemicals that serve as pesticides can be produced by inserting genetic material from bacteria or other organisms into a plant.

This ability to move genes among different species has resulted in the development of plant and animal cells that will glow under ultraviolet light, grow faster, grow taller, produce more chemicals, etc. There are examples of produce that has been genetically modified to provide precursors to Vitamin A – an important vitamin that is limited in poorer countries. A majority of the common GMOs are used in the agricultural sector and include plants grown for food (both for livestock and human consumption). The ability to move genes does not come without concerns to our well-being and the well-being of the environment. As you will see in the Internet resources provided, these concerns are varied and depend on the stakeholders who involved.

For this lesson, the focus is on helping the students figure out the best questions to ask and ways to search for resources to develop an understanding of the issues surrounding GMOs.

LESSON PREPARATION
Science

You will need to purchase a kit such as Wisconsin Fast Plants ® (see Materials section of this lesson for details) early enough so that they will be available on the first day of this lesson (or assemble your own kits). These kits will include all of the materials to grow the plants including seeds, soil, pots, seeds, and watering system. They do not come with lights. Additionally, you should soak bean seeds and place them on paper towels on trays on daily intervals the week before Lesson 1. Prepared slides and microscopes can be gathered the day of the lesson. Students can do their own root squash to look at the cells of the beans provided by the teacher. If you have limited experience making slides, there are multiple websites available that provide instructions. See https://www.youtube.com/watch?v=cH3vjmjMIZ4 for an example for root tip mitosis. You do not need to stain the root tip, but it may be helpful to do so. Care should be taken to use smaller roots so as not to break the coverslip.

Mathematics

N/A

4

English Language Arts

Before the second class, you will need to identify a variety of resources regarding GMOs. These resources should include examples that are both the reliable and unreliable as well relevant and irrelevant for the lesson. You should become familiar with the resources provide and make sure they provide clear examples of why they would or would not be reliable and relevant. To become more familiar with evaluating internet resources, you can do a google search using the key terms "evaluating internet resources" and choosing education sites (have .edu in the URL). Libraries tend to have useful information for evaluating internet resources. You can also go to the following links:

- https://infoguides.gmu.edu/IT104/evaluate

- https://www.library.georgetown.edu/tutorials/research-guides/evaluating-internet-content

- https://lib.nmu.edu/help/resource-guides/subject-guide/evaluating-internet-sources

Social Studies

You should conduct the same resource search that you will require of your students on Days 1-4 before the start of this lesson. This will help you to become aware of the issues your students might encounter. In particular, you should work to identify the key words and phrases you think are useful in finding resources. A few resources are provided in the Internet Resources section found at the end of the lesson.

Safety Considerations

- Students will be planting and observing seeds during this lesson. There are no major safety concerns beyond the need to maintain good hygiene after working with the soil and watering plants with fertilizers.

- Students will be dissecting bean seeds. This only requires students to use forceps and probes. Students should be instructed on safe use of the forceps. Blunt probes should be fine in this exercise, but sharp probes will allow for separating the embryo and separating parts much more easily. If working with these probes, students should be warned about the inappropriate use of probes and to be wary of where they place them.

- Students will be accessing information using the internet. Care should be taken to protect students from accessing internet sites that are inappropriate. Your IT contact person can provide guidance for appropriate search engines. Additionally, they may already have protective measures in place to prevent the students from accessing inappropriate content.

POTENTIAL MISCONCEPTIONS
Science

- Students may not have a clear understanding of the role of the seed – to provide nutrients and appropriate environment for the embryonic plant to grow. Some students may not even consider seeds a living entity.

- Students often mistakenly believe that plants need soil to sprout.

- Students may think that most of the biomass that that the plant produces is from the soil and not from the CO_2 and water.

Mathematics

N/A

English Language Arts

- Students may not recognize what makes a source relevant or reliable. They might think that any website contains accurate information.

- Social Studies

- Students may have little background with GMOs and as a result may multiple incorrect ideas about how GMO's are produced.

- Students may also think that GMO's are like organisms that occur because of a mutation like what they have seen in action and science fiction movies. They may have opinions based on these misconceptions impacted by the popular media.

SAMPLE STRATEGIES FOR DIFFERENTIATING INSTRUCTION WITHIN THIS LESSON
Science

- Content – More advanced can be asked to think more deeply about the activities occurring during development at the cellular level.

- Process – Students that are struggling with coming to appropriate conclusions could use more scaffolded readings that will support them as they develop the understanding of the parts of the seeds and their function.

- Product – All students will be evaluated on their conceptual understanding in their note-book. However, notebooks could be completed in digital format that allows for images and audio recording.

NATIONAL SCIENCE TEACHING ASSOCIATION

English Language Arts

- Process – Providing fewer resources initially for students to examine and consider relevance, reliability, and relevance will provide more support. Focusing on each of these concepts separately will and then returning to the same resources to discuss them will also provide more support. Finally, allowing for multiple opportunities to get feedback on the resource selection assignment would support those students who are progressing more slowly.

- Product – Students can use multiple methods to complete the appropriate resource selection assignment. Additionally, fewer or more resources can be required depending on the students.

Social Studies

- Content – Depending on their level, students could be asked to focus on a specific question, a group of questions or all of the of primary questions identified on Day 1. Different questions may be more or less difficult to answer, depending on the students ability to use the internet, ability to use good search terms and self-regulation.

- Process – Support from the teacher in this activity can range depending on the capability of the students. Teachers can just provide guiding instructions to more capable students. Teachers can provide progressing students with scaffolding such as identify a few search terms for them. For students that need extra guidance, the teacher can model their process for finding a few resources then coach students on how to use those resources to find terms to search for new resources.

- Product – Students can use multiple methods to complete the appropriate resource selection assignment. Additionally, fewer or more resources can be required depending on the students.

LEARNING PLAN COMPONENTS
INTRODUCTORY ACTIVITY/ENGAGEMENT
Science Class – Plant Structure and Function

Day 1: Show students the seeds from Wisconsin Fast Plants ® or the kits you assembled. Explain to students that over the next two weeks they will become plant scientists working to figure out how different conditions influence plant growth and development. Introduce the lab notebooks they will keep describing their findings.

Lead a discussion with students to determine what they know about plants. In particular, ask students to focus on what plants need to grow, develop, reproduce, and ask students what plant structures they know about and how these structures help the plant grow, develop and reproduce.

Students will plant all three of the Wisconsin Fast Plants ® kits in preparation for the coming weeks. Students will record the procedure and make daily observations of their plants in their lab notebooks.

Mathematics Connections

N/A

English Language Arts Connections – Identifying Reliable and Relevant Information on the Internet

Day 2: Discuss the upcoming task of generating a documentary. Discuss what a documentary is and how it requires that the students use information sources to generate the knowledge that will be used to organize and present the information to others. How can they go about identifying relevant and appropriate resources?

Social studies – Building our knowledge of GMOs

Day 1: First Half – Lead a discussion regarding the type of foods the students like to eat, focusing on the type of fruit and vegetables they enjoy. Highlight the fact that many of the fruits and vegetables that we find in the supermarket are not normally found in the wild, but have been generated in a variety of ways. The ways of generating particularly desirable plants for food dates to ancient times when humans began domesticating wild plants (the beginning of agriculture). Explain that we continue to alter these plants by a variety of means, but point out that in the past 20 years a new method has been used.

Introduce the concept of GMOs and show a video describes the GMO issue generally. For instance:

- Why are GMOs Bad? SciShow – https://www.youtube.com/watch?v=sH4bi60alZU – this video does a good job of describing both the issues and what GMOs are. Additionally it is a great example of what the students' documentaries might look like.

- GMO Controversies – Science vs. public fear: Borut Bohanec – https://www.youtube.com/watch?v=mz4_TwdaYeI

- Waiter, there is a gene in my soup!! – Jimmy Botella – https://www.youtube.com/watch?v=Mwzq-swl4cI

- "The Gene Revolution, The Future of Agriculture: Dr. Thierry Vrain at https://www.youtube.com/watch?v=RQkQXyiynYs

- What is a GMO (part 1 – https://youtu.be/Czx8nF7GrIM and part 2 – https://youtu.be/l0LhPz4f1QM these videos provide excellent of genetic modification including genetic engineering and transgenic genes). It does provide a viewpoint that is more positive toward genetic engineering as no more problematic than the other mechanisms we have used to modify genes in organisms in the past.

Lead a discussion after watching the video. Ask students:

- What have you heard about genetically modified foods?

- How can we decide if they are good or bad?

Watch video – from Jimmy Kimmel live video – What's a GMO? – https://www.youtube.com/watch?v=EzEr23XJwFY – highlight the fact that many people know very little about GMOs and yet are making critical choices that involve GMOs on a regular basis.

Introduce the module challenge to students:

YOUR CHALLENGE:

As citizens, it is up to us to determine the pros and cons of new technologies such as genetic engineering. But in order to make informed decisions, we need to understand all sides of the issues associated with these technologies. Over the next several weeks we will be exploring GMOs to develop our understanding in order to better communicate to others what the issues are and what potential solutions might be.

Goal – At the end of the unit, you and your partners will produce a short documentary that examines the pros and cons of the genetic modification of organisms that we eat. These videos will be shared with your peers and members of the community to help them better understand the potential positives and pitfalls of genetically modifying organisms.

Tell students that they will be divided into groups of 3–4 students to work as a documentary team.

Activity/Investigation
Science class – Plant Structure and Function

Days 2-4: Bean Seed Exploration: What is happening to our germinating seeds right now?

Students will examine bean seeds at different stages of germination to figure out what happens as the seeds start to germinate. The focus of this lesson is to have students identify the following:

- parts of the embryonic plant

- germination progress (starting with roots)

- uptake of oxygen during germination

- that seeds only require water to start germinating

- cells

- that cells form tissues (specifically that meristematic tissue produces new cells in plants).

Students should do this with multiple activities in the following order:

Activity 1: What is inside a seed? – Bean seed dissection – examples of dissections can be found in a number of places. In particular, students should focus on the root (radicle), shoots, and leaves:

- https://www.youtube.com/watch?v=pQYJ2PSDu3A

- https://www.youtube.com/watch?v=6_uRLqm8uTA

Activity 2: What is happening to the embryonic plant? – Anatomical changes in seeds as time progresses – Students will look at bean seeds planted at different times and will describe and draw in their notebooks, anatomically what is happening to the embryonic plant over time. They should describe that the roots are extending and hairs are forming around the root. Students can use dissecting microscopes to see more details to describe and diagram.

Activity 3: Is the embryonic plant conducting photosynthesis? – looking at CO2 gas production in the plant. Students can do this using probeware. Simple respirometers can also be used to show that gases are being used instead of being produced. An example can be found at https://www.youtube.com/watch?v=W11U DJnervw.

Activity 4: What does the growing root look like? – looking at root slides. Students can look at slides of roots under the compound scope to describe the structure involved with growing the new roots. In particular students should focus on the meristematic tissue (cells producing new cells) and growth zones (areas where new cells grow larger and elongate). They should also notice that the root hairs are coming from the outer layer.

Mathematics connections

N/A

English Language Arts connections – Identifying Reliable and Relevant Information on the Internet

Day 2: Identifying Reliable and Relevant Information on the Internet
In small groups students will examine various sources focusing on the general issues surrounding GMOs provided by the teacher. Below are a few sample sources focusing on GMOs that are examples of the dichotomy of reliable/unreliable and relevant/not-relevant:

- Grist.org – this source is questionable with its reliability because it is considered to have a moderate liberal bias. Additionally, it is not peer-reviewed. While it might present information in a factual way, it will use prose that are intended to sway toward liberal causes. Additionally, rather than exploring the evidence directly, the articles within this source are largely summarizing the original work but not providing references so that the reader can find and evaluate the evidence themselves. The two articles below are not very relevant as they are more focused on the profits of GMO crops not the safety concerns expressed by many against GMOs.

    a. http://grist.org/food/golden-apple-or-forbidden-fruit-following-the-money-on-gmos/
    b. http://grist.org/food/are-gmos-worth-their-weight-in-gold-to-farmers-not-exactly/

- AAAS.org – this source is a pro-science outlet and is known for factual reporting and is thought to be relatively unbiased, basing decisions on the consensus of the scientific community. The particular article provided is relevant but could be considered unreliable because it takes a particular stance rather than sharing the facts and allowing the reader to make their own decision. However, they do provide references to the two sources of evidence they present allowing the reader to find and evaluate the evidence themselves. http://www.aaas.org/news/statement-aaas-board-directors-labeling-genetically-modified-foods

- Modernfarmer.com – this magazine is a non-peer reviewed and is focused on being "the authoritative resource for today's cutting-edge food producers and consumers. It would be considered less reliable because of not being peer-reviewed. The articles within this source are largely summarizing the original work but not providing references so that the reader can find and evaluate the evidence themselves. This article however would be considered relevant. http://modernfarmer.com/2013/12/post-gmo-economy/

- USDA.gov and gov websites – these sources can be skeptically considered as reliable as it is a government source, given that government can be influenced

by the administrations political perspectives. This particular article, however, is likely both reliable and relevant as it provides factual information based on evidence that can be examined and evaluated by the reader. https://www.ers. usda.gov/webdocs/publications/45179/43667_err162_summary.pdf?v=0

- ISAAA.org – this source might be considered less reliable, as it has a pro-biotechnology stance as indicated on its website. The information provided might be factual, but should be evaluated with the recognition of the inherent bias. This particular website could be considered both reliable and relevant as it is providing a list of approved crops that fall under the genetically engineered category. http://www.isaaa.org/gmapprovaldatabase/default.asp

- EDU websites – sources with the .edu url are thought to be reliable, however, caution should be used as even academics can have a particular bias in their writing. Since this website is NOT peer-reviewed, it should be viewed skeptically as reliable. The purpose of the page is to inform, so it is less of a concern with bias since the reader can search the site to find references. This particular article would be considered relevant because it provides background knowledge for understanding the issue. http://www.bt.ucsd.edu/gmo.html

- Wikipedia – often thought of as unreliable since its content is crowd sourced. This "peer-review" process is not the same as happens in original research articles, but is very similar. It is a useful resource for getting gaining understanding. Additionally, the presence of references allows the reader to go to the original sources to determine if the interpretation of the information is accurate. his article would be considered relevant. https://en.wikipedia.org/wiki/Genetically_modified_crops

- New Republic – this source is considered to be hyper-partisan and liberal (MediaBiasChart.com). It is considered to have selective or incomplete stories and unfair persuasion. This article is relevant, however. https://newrepublic.com/article/135617/gmos-save-lifethey-might-already

- Daily Beast – this source is also considered to be hyper-partisan and conservative (MediaBiasChart.com). The articles are known to be suitable for analysis not or reporting facts directly. https://www.thedailybeast.com/were-paranoid-about-gmo-foods-because-of-pseudo-science

- Natural News – advocates for a natural lifestyle free of synthetic chemicals. They "criticizes drugs-and-surgery medicine, vaccines, corporate corruption, animal testing, the use of humans for medical experiments, the chemical contamination of foods, heavy metals in consumer products, factory farming and government corruption. Natural News also warns its readers about science gone bad and frequently cites examples of science resulting in catastrophes that it calls 'crimes' against humanity." (from https://www. naturalnews.com/About.html). This particular article would be considered relevant but biased. https://www.naturalnews.com/053487_GMOs_crop_ yields_genetic_diversity.html

Students will decide as a group which sources are relevant and reliable for getting the basic information for their documentary.

Day 3: In small groups students will examine various sources focusing on the general issues surrounding GMOs provided by the teacher. They will decide as a group how to identify the relevant information within the source and how to take notes on the resources for use in synthesizing their knowledge of GMO issues.

Social Studies Class – Building Our Knowledge of GMOs

Day 1 (second half) to Day 5: Lead a discussion with students to determine what information they should have to in be better informed on GMOs. Specifically focus the students on the following types of information:

- What is a GMO? How are they created?

- What are examples of GMOs that currently exist?

- Who stand to profit or lose with the GMOs? (who are the stakeholders?)

- What are possible benefits from GMOs in agriculture?

- What are possible threats from GMOs in agriculture?

Students should discuss ways in which they could get the information they have identified as important. Offer specific search engine and key words, help students recognize that each article will provide new key words for their search, and encourage students to recognize the most important information in each source. Over the next three days, students will be looking for resources and working to get answers to the questions above. Students should be reminded that the focus of this search is not to decide whether GMOs are good or bad, but rather is to gather information to be used in making that decision at a later date. Students should have their resources and answer to these questions by the start of Day 5.

Explain

Science class – Plant Structure and Function

Day 5: What is the role of the roots, and how do plants grow? Students should discuss the order in which they observe the plant grow and develop. Encourage students to consider why the root grows first. Students will conduct a webquest to answer the

following in their STEM research notebooks (under the heading Root Structure and Function – Webquest):

- What is the function of the root? How does the root anatomy help the root to perform this function?

- What is happening to help the root grow?

- What is the definition of tissue in multicellular organisms like plants?

- What are some examples of tissues that are found in the root and what is their function?

After students have completed the webquest, lead a discussion using these questions to verify that students have appropriate answers.

Students should be able to explain the plant structures they see and relate them to their general functions (roots bringing in water and providing support for plant; stems providing support for leaves and transit between root and leaves; leaves as the site of photosynthesis). In their observations students should describe how the roots are growing (i.e., by producing new cells at the root tip and elongating them, allowing the root to stretch). They should be able to relate that the root provides support as well obtaining water and nutrients from the soil. Likewise, the root hairs they observe are useful in anchoring the root but also help get more water from the soil. Students should also gain an understanding that areas of cells that function for a particular purpose are called tissue. The cells in the root make up the epidermal tissue that protect the root as it pushes through the soil, the vascular tissue that moves water and nutrients to and from the roots, and the meristematic tissue where cell division is the primary function. Students should also recognize that all of these tissues work together to set up the new plant so it can grow upward toward light and perform photosynthesis.

Mathematics connections

N/A

English Language Arts connections – Identifying Reliable and Relevant Information on the Internet

Day 2: Identifying Reliable and Relevant Information on the Internet (continued)

Facilitate a discussion in which students create a set of rules for determining appropriate resources for gathering information on an issue. Specifically, students should recognize whether the resource provides information that specifically focuses on the questions identified in social studies. They should also understand that the source of the information should be evaluated to determine whether it can be trusted. Further, students should understand that there is typically not one ultimate source of any information, but information often will come from synthesizing multiple sources of reliable and trusted information. Using the set of rules the class developed, students will examine the resources they identified in their searches and determine whether they are or are not each source is appropriate for use in their documentary. Students will be providing a list of six resources that they have identified as appropriate or not appropriate, explaining briefly why a resource was considered placed in each category.

Day 3: Identifying Reliable and Relevant Information on the Internet (continued)

Facilitate a discussion in which students discuss how to read and identify relevant information within a set of readings provided by the teacher and how to summarize the information for future communication. Students should focus on identifying key words and phrases and building a vocabulary list around the issue. They should also be able to summarize important ideas within a reading rather than using direct quotes. This is a good place to discuss with students the importance of citing sources and the concept of plagiarism. Students should implement these strategies using one of the resources they identified for the GMO exploration and provide a set of summary notes that highlight the important ideas. Additionally, students should create a current vocabulary list (with definitions) of words and phrases they are encountering that need to be clarified to better understand the topic.

Social Studies Class – Building Our Knowledge of GMOs

Day 5: Building our Knowledge of GMOs (continued)

Lead a discussion focused on the answers students found for the questions (see Day 1, social studies). Focus on the definition of a GMO and the stakeholders in the GMO issue, ensuring that students understand that there are multiple definitions of GMOs that may be used, depending on the stakeholder. Students should be able to state that scientists consider an organism as genetically modified if their genes have been genetically manipulated to include specific DNA from a different organism. This might include genes from the same species or closely related species (cisgenic) or genes from a completely different species that would not combine naturally (transgenic). Further, students should also recognize that stakeholders for the agricultural GMO issue include scientists, farmers, business owners, and consumers, government agencies, other countries, etc. They should also see that depending on the groups' viewpoint regarding GMOs, each of these stakeholder groups could stand to gain or lose with the increasing use of GMOs. The benefits and threats differ depending on the purpose of the GMO. Table 4.3 provides a list of potential benefits and costs for a variety of stakeholders. This is not intended to be an exhaustive list but primarily as a potential starting point for teachers to start the discussion with students. There may be other costs and benefits that are not listed that are just as valid and might be introduced by the students.

Table 4.3. Table of Potential Benefits and Costs for Each Stakeholder

Stakeholder	Benefit	Costs
Scientists	Enhanced tools for addressing societal issues such as disease, nutritional deficiencies, environmental contamination	Focus on GMOs as a "magic bullet" may result in less focus on alternative approaches that might be just as safe and cost effective.
Farmers	Increased crop yield, decreased pesticide or herbicide use, reduce usage of water, etc.	Increasing pesticide and herbicide resistance in environment, higher cost of seeds, potential negative perception from community
Business	Varied, depending on the business – for groceries, GMOs allow for less waste (produce may stay fresh longer, allowing longer transit times and shelf life), more availability	Negative perception from the community when the GMOs are allowed
Consumers	Potential for greater nutrient/ vitamin gain, potential lower costs, potential lower impact to environment	Possible long-term health impacts not yet studied

Extend/Apply Knowledge
Science connections

N/A

Mathematics connections

N/A

English Language Arts connections – Identifying Reliable and Relevant Information on the Internet

Days 4–5: Identifying Reliable and Relevant Information on the Internet (continued)

Working in groups, students should take the information they collected in their search during social studies to summarize GMOs and the issues surrounding their use in agriculture in two written pages.

Social Studies class

N/A

Evaluate/Assessment

Performance Tasks – see attached rubrics for each of these tasks

1. Class participation rubric – Students will participate in whole class discussions, making claims that are backed up by evidence and reasoning.

2. Appropriate resource selection assignment – Students will provide a list of their resources for the information they have gathered, indicating which resource was used to answer which question. Further, they will include a short statement for that explains why they think the source is appropriate to use (relevant and reliable).

3. Summarized learning assignment – Students will provide evidence that they are using effective techniques to build knowledge regarding GMOs.

4. Student STEM research notebook – students will keep research notebooks with entries regarding their experiment as well as answers to questions from webquests.

Other Measures – see attached rubrics for each of these tasks

1. Summary of GMO – Students will summarize the GMO issue by providing answers to the questions initially identified in social studies on the first day.

INTERNET RESOURCES
Science Resources

- http://www.plantingscience.org/index.php?module=content&func=view&pid=117

- http://www.carolina.com/wfp-plant-growth-and-development/exploring-variation-with-wisconsin-fast-plants-kit/158706.pr?question=

- http://www.carolina.com/wfp-genetics/wisconsin-fast-plants-irradiated-seed-kit/FAM_158750.pr?question=

- http://www.carolina.com/wfp-environmental-science/wisconsin-fast-plants-nutrition-study-kit/FAM_158720.pr?question=#family-details

- https://www.youtube.com/watch?v=cH3vjmjMIZ4

- https://www.youtube.com/watch?v=pQYJ2PSDu3A

- https://www.youtube.com/watch?v=6_uRLqm8uTA

- https://www.youtube.com/watch?v=W11UDJnervw

English Language Arts Resources

- http://www.skillsyouneed.com/write/notes-reading.html
- http://www.scholastic.com/teachers/article/grades-6-8-activities-teach-note-taking
- http://www.educationworld.com/a_lesson/lesson/lesson322.shtml

Social Studies Resources

- https://www.youtube.com/watch?v=sH4bi60alZU
- https://www.youtube.com/watch?v=mz4_TwdaYeI
- https://www.youtube.com/watch?v=Mwzq-swl4cI
- https://www.youtube.com/watch?v=RQkQXyiynYs
- https://www.youtube.com/watch?v=EzEr23XJwFY

Some resources for GMO search

- http://grist.org/food/golden-apple-or-forbidden-fruit-following-the-money-on-gmos/
- http://www.aaas.org/news/statement-aaas-board-directors-labeling-genetically-modified-foods
- http://grist.org/food/are-gmos-worth-their-weight-in-gold-to-farmers-not-exactly/
- http://modernfarmer.com/2013/12/post-gmo-economy/
- http://www.ers.usda.gov/publications/err-economic-research-report/err162/report-summary.aspx
- http://www.isaaa.org/gmapprovaldatabase/default.asp
- http://www.bt.ucsd.edu/gmo.html
- https://en.wikipedia.org/wiki/Genetically_modified_crops

Class Participation Rubric

Characteristic	Emerging (1)	Proficient (2)	Exemplary (3)
Follows guidelines of intellectual discussion and is civil	Criticizes other people personally instead of being critical of ideas; doesn't use appropriate language	Challenges the idea but without reason; uses appropriate language	Challenges the idea with solid reasoning; uses appropriate language; diverts any unproductive discussion
Makes claim	Claim unoriginal AND indirectly related to topic	Claim original AND indirectly related to topic	Claim original AND directly related to topic
Uses reliable sources for evidence	Uses unreliable resources (such as Wikipedia or blog)	Only uses textbook as resource	Uses outside reliable resources (such as a scientific journal or .gov or .edu website)
Appropriate level of evidence	Opinion-based evidence	One piece of researched evidence	More than one piece of researched evidence
Responds to the content of the discussion	No response or unrelated to claim	Response is indirectly associated with claim	Response is aligned with claim
Connects with what prior person says	Unrelated to current discussion	Stay on topic, but makes no connection with person before them	Acknowledges prior person's idea and elaborates on what previous person says
Able to defend their claim/rebuttal	Has no response	Has a response but cannot back up response	Has a response and is able to back up response with further evidence
Uses appropriate reasoning	Reasoning is disconnected from claim	Reasoning is superficially connected to claim	Reasoning directly connects claim to evidence

Appropriate Resources Selection Assignment Rubric

	Beginning	Progressing	Advanced
Reliable Sources	Students resources are not accurately classified as reliable or not reliable AND The discussion regarding why the sources are reliable do not provide a clear focus on any of the following: source or author, date the source was produced, the depth of the information within the source	Students resources are accurately classified as reliable or not reliable BUT The discussion regarding why the sources are reliable do not provide a clear focus on any of the following: source or author, date the source was produced, the depth of the information within the source OR Students resources are not accurately classified as reliable or not reliable BUT Discussion regarding why the sources are or are not reliable focus on any of the following: source or author, date the source was produced, the depth of the information within the source	Students resources are accurately classified as reliable or not reliable AND Discussion regarding why the sources are or are not reliable focus on any of the following: source or author, date the source was produced, the depth of the information within the source
Relevant Sources	Students resources are not accurately classified as relevant or not relevant AND Discussion regarding why the sources are or are not relevant does not focus on the depth of the information within the source or the connection between the content and the topic	Students resources are accurately classified as relevant or not relevant BUT Discussion regarding why the sources are or are not relevant does not focus on the depth of the information within the source or the connection between the content and the topic OR Students resources are not accurately classified as relevant or not relevant BUT Discussion regarding why the sources are or are not relevant focus on the depth of the information within the source or the connection between the content and the topic	Students resources are accurately classified as relevant or not relevant AND Discussion regarding why the sources are or are not relevant focus on the depth of the information within the source or the connection between the content and the topic

NOTE: Modify rubric as needed to include rules identified through discussion.

Summarized Learning Assignment Rubric

	Beginning	Progressing	Advanced
Vocabulary	List is limited or contains limited or inaccurate definitions AND List includes items irrelevant to the topic, including terms and phrases that are not associated with GMOs	List is extensive and includes accurate definitions AND List includes items irrelevant to the topic, including terms and phrases that are not associated with GMOs OR List is limited or contains limited or inaccurate definitions AND List is relevant to the topic, focusing on terms and phrases that are clearly associated with GMOs	List is extensive and includes accurate definitions AND List is relevant to the topic, focusing on terms and phrases that are clearly associated with GMOs
Identifying main ideas	Ideas provided are tangential to the topic	Accurately identifies some of the main ideas from the reading OR Includes some ideas that are tangential to the topic	Accurately identifies all of the main ideas from the reading
Using summaries	All of the notes provided appear to be taken verbatim from the text	Some of the notes provided are summaries, others appear to be taken verbatim from the text	All notes are summaries
Quality of summaries	Most summaries are limited in capturing the ideas in the text	Some summaries are limited in capturing the ideas in the text	All summaries effectively capture the ideas in the text

NOTE: Modify rubric as needed to include rules identified through discussion.

STEM Research Notebook Rubric

	Beginning	Progressing	Advanced
Entries Related to Experimental Design			
Methods	Methods incomplete	Description of methods for planting seeds is clearly indicated BUT How each set of seeds were treated differently is not clear	Description of methods for planting seeds is clearly indicated AND How each set of seeds were treated differently within a particular experiment is clearly indicated
Raw Data	Daily data absent	Daily data present, but not easily found	Daily data are clearly indicated
Summarized Data	Data not organized in tables	Data organized in tables but no labels to indicate	Data organized in tables with clear labels for each column and row
Entries Related to Webquests			
Vocabulary	No vocabulary is used OR Vocabulary is not defined	Writing uses some vocabulary to convey the ideas OR Vocabulary isn't always defined	Writing effectively uses appropriate vocabulary to convey the ideas AND Vocabulary is defined
Use of facts and details	Few facts and details are provided	Facts and details chosen are not always appropriate for communicating ideas	Facts and details chosen are appropriate and effectively communicating the ideas
Use of examples	No examples are provided OR Examples do not communicate the ideas	Examples are provided to support ideas BUT Examples provided are too few OR Examples provided do not always effectively communicate the ideas	Examples are provided to support ideas AND All examples provided effectively communicate the ideas
Syntax	Uses poor sentence structure	Student mostly uses appropriate sentence structure	Student uses appropriate sentence structure
Overall Organization	Organization is lacking	Organization is apparent, but is not effective in building understanding of the topic	Organization effectively builds understanding of the topic
Answers Questions	Fewer than 3 questions are answered thoroughly	3 of the 4 questions are answered thoroughly	All questions are answered thoroughly

GMO Summary Assignment Rubric

	Beginning	Progressing	Advanced
Vocabulary	No vocabulary is used OR Vocabulary is not defined	Writing uses some vocabulary to convey the ideas OR Vocabulary isn't always defined	Writing effectively uses appropriate vocabulary to convey the ideas AND Vocabulary is defined
Use of facts and details	Few facts and details are provided	Facts and details chosen are not always appropriate for communicating the ideas	Facts and details chosen are appropriate, effectively communicating the ideas
Use of examples	No examples are provided OR Examples do not communicate the ideas	Examples are provided to support ideas BUT Examples provided are too few OR Examples provided do not always effectively communicate the ideas	Examples are provided to support ideas AND All examples provided effectively communicate the ideas
Syntax	Uses poor sentence structure	Student mostly uses appropriate sentence structure	Student uses appropriate sentence structure
Overall Organization	Organization is lacking	Organization is apparent, but is not effective for building understanding of the topic	Organization effectively builds understanding of the topic
Defining GMO	Definition of GMO is not included	Students can accurately define a GMO	Students can accurately define a GMO
Stakeholders	Does not identify stakeholders OR Does not explain how stakeholders are impacted by the issue	Identifies all stakeholders involved BUT Does not explain how they are impacted by the issue OR Identifies some stakeholders involved BUT Explains how they are impacted by the issue	Identifies all stakeholders involved AND Explains how they are impacted by the issue

Continued

GMO Summary Assignment Rubric (*continued*)

	Beginning	Progressing	Advanced
Benefits of GMO	Limited benefits are identified AND Benefits are not clearly supported with examples	Identifies multiple benefits BUT Benefits are not clearly supported with examples OR Limited benefits are identified BUT Benefits are clearly supported with examples	Identifies multiple benefits AND Benefits are clearly supported with examples
Threats of GMO	Limited threats are identified AND Threats are not clearly supported with examples	Identifies multiple threats BUT Threats are not clearly supported with examples OR Limited threats are identified BUT Threats are clearly supported with examples	Identifies multiple threats AND Threats are clearly supported with examples

Lesson Plan 2: How Do We Make Decisions About GMOs?

LESSON SUMMARY

In social studies, students will begin to examine ways in which individuals and communities makes decisions regarding GMOs. The concept of cost-benefit analyses will be introduced, and students will use the evaluation of pros and cons to come to a decision regarding their position about the use of GMOs in agriculture.

Students will explore author viewpoint in non-fiction writing, specifically examining the arguments around GMOs from a variety of different perspectives. Additionally, students will focus on the claims, evidence and reasoning used in pro and con arguments.

In science, students will continue exploring the anatomy and physiology of vascular plants, focusing on the stem and leaves and their function and on the tissue and cells involved in the leaves and stems. Finally, students will begin the transition into thinking about how the environment might influence the anatomy (and potentially the function) of a plant.

ESSENTIAL QUESTION(S)

Science

- What is the role of the stem and how does its structure allow it to perform its function?

- What is the role of leaf and how does its structure allow it to perform its function?

- How do the stem and leaves grow?

Mathematics

- What is a cost/benefit analysis?

- How can a cost/benefit analysis be used to determine if using GMOs in agriculture is a good idea?

English Language/Arts

- What makes compelling arguments?

- How does someone's perspective influence what arguments they might find compelling?

- How do we decide if GMOs are good or bad?

ESTABLISHED GOALS/OBJECTIVES
Science

- Explain the function of the root, stem and leaf of a plant.

- Describe the role of the meristematic tissue, epidermal tissue, and vascular tissue in the stem and leaves.

- Describe the anatomical features that allow leaves to perform photosynthesis.

Mathematics

- Determine the inputs and outputs for a cost-benefit analysis.

- Use cost-benefit analysis to evaluate the economic viability of GMOs.

- Use the engineering design process to develop a potential process to prevent GMO contamination into organic crops.

English Language Arts

- Identify claims, evidence, and reasoning within an argument.

- Create an argument that contains at least one claim with its supporting evidence and reasoning.

Social Studies

- Describe how the viewpoint of an individual will influence what arguments are compelling.

- Describe ways to compromise such that all stakeholders' viewpoints are considered.

- Use cost-benefit analysis as a way to evaluate pros and cons of an issue.

TIME REQUIRED – 5 DAYS
NECESSARY MATERIALS
Science

- Days 6–9

  o   Bean sprouts and young bean plants should be available for students to explore.

- Day 10

  o Computers with Internet access for groups of students. Optional: provide a list of starting sites or key words for students.

Mathematics

- Days 6–7

  o Some method of performing calculations such as a spreadsheet or calculator.

- Days 7–10

  o Computers with Internet access for groups of students.

English Language Arts

- Days 6–8
  o Computers with Internet access for groups of students.
  o Example resources intended for persuading the reader toward a particular stance.
  o Argumentation Graphic Organizer (attached at the end of this lesson).

Social Studies

- Days 6–10

  o Computers with Internet access for groups of students.

Table 4.4. Standards Addressed in STEM Road Map Module Lesson Two

NEXT GENERATION SCIENCE STANDARDS PERFORMANCE OBJECTIVES MS-LS1–3 – Use argument supported by evidence for how the body is a system of interacting subsystems composed of groups of cells. DISCIPLINARY CORE IDEAS AND CROSSCUTTING CONCEPTS LS1.A: Structure and Function – In multicellular organisms, the body is a system of multiple interacting subsystems. These subsystems are groups of cells that work together to form tissues and organs that are specialized for particular body functions. (MS-LS1-3) LS1.B: Growth and Development of Organisms – Organisms reproduce, either sexually or asexually, and transfer their genetic information to their offspring (secondary to MSLS3-2)

Continued

Table 4.4. (*continued*)

Science and Engineering Practices

CONSTRUCTING EXPLANATIONS AND DESIGNING SOLUTIONS – Constructing explanations and designing solutions in 6–8 builds on K–5 experiences and progresses to include constructing explanations and designing solutions supported by multiple sources of evidence consistent with scientific ideas, principles, and theories. Apply scientific ideas to construct an explanation for realworld phenomena, examples, or events. (MS-LS4–2); Construct an explanation that includes qualitative or quantitative relationships between variables that describe phenomena (MS-LS4–4)

OBTAINING, EVALUATING, AND COMMUNICATING INFORMATION – Obtaining, evaluating, and communicating information in 6–8 builds on K–5 experiences and progresses to evaluating the merit and validity of ideas and methods. Gather, read, and synthesize information from multiple appropriate sources and assess the credibility, accuracy, and possible bias of each publication and methods used, and describe how they are supported or not supported by evidence (MS-LS4–5)

COMMON CORE MATHEMATICS STANDARDS

MATHEMATICS PRACTICES

MP1 – Make sense of problems and persevere in solving them.
MP3 – Construct viable arguments and critique the reasoning of others.

Mathematics Content

7.RP.A.2 – Recognize and represent proportional relationships between quantities.
7.RP.A.2.C – Represent proportional relationships by equations. For example, if total cost is proportional to the number n of items purchased at a constant price p, the relationship between the total cost and the number of items can be expressed as t = pn.
7.NS.A.1 – Apply and extend previous understandings of addition and subtraction to add and subtract rational numbers; represent addition and subtraction on a horizontal or vertical number line diagram.
7.NS.A.1.D – Apply properties of operations as strategies to add and subtract rational numbers.
7.NS.A.3 – Solve real-world and mathematical problems involving the four operations with rational numbers (computations with rational numbers extend the rules for manipulating fractions to complex fractions).

COMMON CORE ENGLISH LANGUAGE ARTS STANDARDS

WRITING STANDARDS

W.7.1.A – Introduce claim(s), acknowledge alternate or opposing claims, and organize the reasons and evidence logically.
W.7.1.B – Support claim(s) with logical reasoning and relevant evidence, using accurate, credible sources and demonstrating an understanding of the topic or text.
W.7.1.C – Use words, phrases, and clauses to create cohesion and clarify the relationships among claim(s), reasons, and evidence.
W.7.1.E – Provide a concluding statement or section that follows from and supports the argument presented.

Table 4.4. (*continued*)

Reading Standards

RI.7.8 – Trace and evaluate the argument and specific claims in a text, assessing whether the reasoning is sound and the evidence is relevant and sufficient to support the claims.

RI.7.9 – Analyze how two or more authors writing about the same topic shape their presentations of key information by emphasizing different evidence or advancing different interpretations of facts.

21ST CENTURY SKILLS

Environmental Literacy, Financial, Economic, Business and Entrepreneurial literacy, Critical Thinking and Problem Solving, Information Literacy

Table 4.5. Key Vocabulary for Lesson Two

Key Vocabulary	Definition
Claim	An explanation that answers a question or problem
Cost-Benefit Analysis	An approach to systematically examine the potential positives and negatives related to a particular strategy. This is especially useful in making financial decisions
Evidence	The summarized data or set of facts on which the claim is based
Reasoning	A rule or principle that describes why the evidence supports the claim
Stakeholders	Individuals with an interest or concern in an issue. These are individuals that are impacted (negatively or positively, directly or indirectly) by the issue and therefore may have a particular stance or perspective

TEACHER BACKGROUND INFORMATION
Science

Students will explore their plants' growth as well as the structure and function of stems and leaves during this week. By the end of the week, students should understand the concept of tissues and systems in plants. Additionally, they will see how similar cells may be found in different locations, but still have similar functions. Students will also start thinking about how a plant can change growth patterns in each of the major plant organs (roots, stems, and leaves) in response to the environment.

Mathematics

Simple mathematics associated with cost-benefit analysis

English Language Arts

Students will need to understand the basics of argumentation. If you are not familiar with the basic format of claims, evidence, and reasoning in an argument, you can learn more at the following websites:

- http://www.edutopia.org/blog/science-inquiry-claim-evidence-reasoning-eric-brunsell

- https://www.teachingchannel.org/videos/support-claims-with-evidence-getty

- https://www.youtube.com/watch?v=fkpZfpNWjWY

Social Studies

It is important in this lesson that students be familiar with the stakeholders associated with the production and use of GMOs. The various perspectives of these stakeholder groups plays an important role in determine what arguments groups might find compelling. Additionally, during the last two class periods, students will try to come to a class consensus regarding a position on GMOs. It is important to help students recognize all perspectives from the stakeholders as well as to encourage students to compromise.

LESSON PREPARATION
Science

You should purchase or grow bean sprouts and young bean plants early enough to be available on the first day of this lesson.

Safety Considerations

- Students will be accessing information using the internet. Care should be taken to protect students from accessing internet sites that are inappropriate. Your IT contact person can provide guidance for appropriate search engines. Additionally, they may already have protective measures in place to prevent the students from accessing inappropriate content.

POTENTIAL MISCONCEPTIONS
Science

- Students may believe that the only purpose of the stem is to support the leaves and get them closer to the light. They also care water to and from the roots.

- Students may not be aware that plants not only do photosynthesis but also do cellular respiration. Plants are not doing photosynthesis for our benefit but for their own.

Mathematics

- Students may think that they can always quantify the costs and benefits.

English Language Arts

- Students may think that arguments are emotional and personal.

- Students may perceive claims without evidence or weak evidence to be just as effective as claims with strong evidence.

Social Studies

N/A

SAMPLE STRATEGIES FOR DIFFERENTIATION IN THIS LESSON

Science

- Content – More advanced can be asked to think more deeply about the actions of the stem and leaf tissue at the cellular level. Websites that show the basic structure and function of roots, stems and leaves can be used to support students, such as https://www.ck12.org/book/CK-12-Biology/section/16.2/

- Process – Students that are struggling with coming to appropriate conclusions could use more scaffolded readings that will support them as they develop the understanding of the function of the stem and leaves.

- Product – All students will be evaluated on their conceptual understanding in their note-book. However, notebooks could be completed in digital format that allows for images and audio recording. Products could be differentiated along a range of recording basic knowledge of stems, roots, and leaves to a complex argument demonstrating how similar plant structures, even at different locations, have the same function.

Mathematics

- Content – The basic content will be the same, regardless of student level, but some students may be able to be more sophisticated in their identification of inputs and outputs.

- Process – Provide more examples of cost-benefit analyses. Breaking down the steps to identifying the input type, input cost, output type, output cost, and

difference between input and output cost could provide those students who struggle with more support.

- Product – Students can be asked to include more or less input and output in their cost-benefit analysis.

English Language Arts

- Content – Some students may need to write arguments in a formulaic way while more advanced students may be able to write more sophisticated arguments that include counter arguments and rebuttals that reference their research.

- Process – Students who are struggling with the task can be provided selected resources that clearly state the claim and evidence for them to use in the argument. Teachers can also model how to unpack an argument for students in the readings they provide.

- Product – Students who have difficulty writing their arguments could communicate the argument assignment using digital platforms in audio or video arguments. Alternatively, students could directly report their arguments to their teacher for feedback, focusing on each part of the argument one at a time. The argument graphic organizer can also be scaffolded for the student by providing parts of the arguments and require students to complete the rest.

Social Studies

- Process – Teachers can provide modeling or scaffolding to address the activities in this lesson for more support. Modeling might include taking a specific stakeholders viewpoint and describing how to approach determining their view and how that might influence arguments used and how solutions offered might be accepted. Scaffolding could include providing some written questions such as "What would be the benefit of impact of GMO's to this person's life?", "Why would they want or not want GMO's?", "What would convince them that your solution is feasible?"

LEARNING PLAN COMPONENTS
INTRODUCTORY ACTIVITY/ENGAGEMENT
Science class – Plant Structure and Function

Day 6: Students make observations of the plants they started in Lesson 1. Students will start to see that their plants are now starting to produce secondary growth and they can imagine that the roots are still growing in the soil. Ask students to consider the other structures they saw in their embryonic bean seed. Just like the roots, each serves a function and students will figure out what those functions are.

Mathematics connections – Economy of GMOs

Day 6: Lead a discussion with the students as follows: "You've been exploring GMO's in your other classes. One of the questions in agriculture is whether GMOs make more economic sense. How could we figure that out?" Have students brainstorm ideas to solve the problem (encourage students to come to a relatively common explanation involving determining the costs of inputs and income from outputs). Ask students to consider what mathematical procedures they must perform to solve the problem.

English Language Arts connections – Arguments

Day 6: Lead a discussion regarding what would make a compelling argument for or against homework. Discuss stakeholder perspective on the value of an argument.

Social Studies class – Ethics of GMOs

Day 6: Watch the following video about glowing plants: https://www.youtube.com/watch?v=YxFQ9MkwbDs. In 2017, the company in this video has announced that it was no longer pursuing this project because of the biotech challenges they faced getting plants to grow brightly enough. More information can be found at https://www.wired.com/story/inside-the-glowing-plant-startup-that-just-gave-up-its-quest/ regarding the decision to stop pursuing this. Discuss with students that there are people who are currently creating GMOs for a variety of purposes. Ask students:

- Should this be allowed?

- Should we stop it?

- Are there ways that we can have GMOs and still balance the concerns of those who oppose GMOs?

ACTIVITY/INVESTIGATION
Science class – Plant Structure and Function

Days 6–9: Plant Structure and Function (continued)

Students will examine bean seedlings and young bean plant to understand the following:

- The role of the stem and leaves in plants

- Stem and leaf growth and development

- Differences in plant cells in different regions of the plant (chloroplasts more prominent in leaves, etc.).

Students can do this with multiple activities in any order. They should list each of the questions below in their STEM research notebooks and provide a description, drawing, and statement of what they observe that answers the questions:

- Where is growth occurring to allow stems and leaves to get bigger? (Students will examine slides of plants apical meristems under the compound scope to describe the structure involved with growing stems and leaves. They should recognize that these are similar to what they saw in the roots.)

- How are roots, stems, and leaves different and similar? (Students will examine slides of roots, stems, and leaves to describe similarities and differences they find.)

- What Is the plant doing? – Anatomical changes in seeds as time progresses (Students will look at bean seeds planted at different times and will describe and draw in their notebooks, anatomically what is happening to the embryonic plant over time. They should describe that the roots is extending and hairs are forming around the root. They can use dissecting microscope to see more details to describe and diagram.)

- What parts of the plant perform photosynthesis? – looking at gas production in the plant. (Students can take apart a bean seedling and test different parts to see if they are producing oxygen faster than it is consumed – students can do this using probeware or, alternatively, simple respirometers can be used to show that gases are being produced or used.)

Mathematics connections – Economy of GMOs

Days 6–7: Economy of GMOs (continued)

Using data on the costs of GMO crops versus no GMO crops, students will work in groups to identify which data are most important and then analyze the numbers. In particular, students should recognize that the cost of seeds themselves is not a good comparison as it does not take into consideration the potential savings in pesticides or herbicides. Additionally, the potential yield that would go to market might differ. Therefore, a better comparison would be to identify all of the inputs (everything that costs money, time, or effort) to the farmer and then determine the outputs (total crop produce, sale price of crops, etc.). Additionally, this should be standardized to a common measurement when comparing non-GMO crops versus GMO crops. The website listed below provides a great example of an individual conducting a cost-benefit analysis for their farm. Students can label input and output; if the net differences are not provided, students can then do the actual analysis themselves.

Data can be obtained from a website such as the following: http://thefoodiefarmer. blogspot.com/search?updated-min=2014-01-01T00:00:00-08:00&updated-max=2015-01-01T00:00:00-08:00&max-results=16.

English Language Arts connections – Arguments

Day 6: In small groups students will examine multiple sources regarding various groups' stances regarding GMOs. You should choose these resources to show examples of communications to persuade (see Internet Resources sections). Guide students to recognize the use of argumentation focusing on claims, evidence, and reasoning.

Days 7–8: In small groups students will re-examine the sources regarding the GMOs you provided them in Day 6. Using the argumentation graphic organizer (attached at the end of this lesson), they will identify the claims, evidence, and reasoning in each. Guide students to recognize the use of argumentation focusing on claims, evidence, and reasoning.

Social Studies class – Ethics of GMOs

Days 6–8: Students work in teams to focus on specific GMO examples and identify pros and cons of each.

Day 9: Students examine the cost/benefit analysis from Mathematics regarding GMOs – discuss how the information can be useful and discuss what other factors might come into play when making decisions whether to support or oppose GMOs.

EXPLAIN

Science class – Plant Structure and Function

Day 10: What is the role of the stem and leaves? Students will conduct a webquest to answer the following questions in their STEM research notebooks (under the heading Stem and Leaf Structure and Function Webquest):

- What tissue is involved in producing new stem and leaves? Where is it located?

- What is the function of the stem?

- How does the stem anatomy help it perform this function?

- What tissues are present in both the root and stem? Why would they be in both locations? How are the tissues similar or different?

- What is the function of the leaves?

- How does the leaf anatomy help it perform this function?

- What tissues are present in root, stem and leaves? Why would they be in all of these locations? How are the tissues similar or different?

After students have completed the webquest, can lead a discussion of these questions to verify that students have appropriate answers.

Mathematics connections – Economy of GMOs

Day 8: Students present their cost/benefit analysis to the class using a data table and come to a conclusion about the economic impacts of GMOs. After sharing, the teacher should explain to the class that there is an ongoing concern regarding cross-contamination between GMO and non-GMO plants (something of special concern for organic farmers that cannot market their foods if it contains GE DNA. Students should explore the extent of this controversy by examining the following websites and summarizing their findings in their STEM Research Notebook:

- Protecting organic seeds from GMO Contamination – This article highlights some of the concerns, explanations, along with a link to the Organic Seed Growers and Trade Associations workbook to guide organic farmers in avoiding GE contamination. https://www.ecowatch.com/protecting-organic-seeds-from-gmo-contamination-1881929042.html

- Who's Responsible for GMO Contamination? – This article highlights the concerns and potential regulations that might be used to protect non-GMO farmers from contamination. https://seedalliance.org/2014/whos-responsible-for-gmo-contamination/

- Organic Farmers Pay the Price for GMO Contamination – This article provides another negative look at the impacts of GMO contamination, but includes summarized data from farmers. https://www.foodandwaterwatch.org/sites/default/files/GMO%20Contamination%20Farmers%20IB%20March%202014_0.pdf

- Are you a farmer worried about GMO contamination? USDA Says "Get Insurance" – news article from 2012 that summarizes the debate. https://grist.org/food/are-you-a-farmer-worried-about-gmo-contamination-usda-says-get-insurance/

- Coexistence Resources and Statistical Data – Web page from the US Department of Agriculture provides a variety of resources that is intended to promote co-existence among all sectors of agriculture. https://www.usda.gov/topics/farming/coexistence/coexistence-resources-and-statistical-data

- GMO Contamination Prevention: What Does it Take – article that highlights how different sectors of agriculture might co-exist to reduce contamination from GMO. https://demeter-usa.org/downloads/GMO-Contamination-Prevention.pdf

English Language Arts connections – Arguments

Day 9: Hold a class discussion about how the viewpoints of the stakeholders will influence the type of arguments that are considered compelling.

Social Studies class – Ethics of GMOs

Day 9: Have students orally present their findings of pros and cons of GMOs to the class. They will also discuss the role that different disciplines play in providing information to help people make decisions about GMOs.

EXTEND/APPLY KNOWLEDGE
Science class – Plant Structure and Function

Day 10: Lead a discussion to have the students describe how the entire plant structure down to the tissue level and how the plant structure is organized to allow the plant to survive.

In order to get students to think about how the environment might influence the growth of a plant, assign the students with the following homework assignment: provide an argument for how a plant could respond if it were in found below a tree that blocked much of the sun's light. How would the plant's response need to change in terms the systems of the plant that support it.

Responses may include the following: the plant could grow longer stems to reach light, requiring that the vascular system to be longer to move water to the leaves and then nutrients from the leaves to the rest of the cells in the plant. These conditions would also require the roots to be more spread out or deeper to support the plant and keep it from falling over, and the roots would need to bring in more water and minerals. The cells would also need to have thicker cell walls to give the stem more support. Alternatively, the plant could grow broader leaves to extend the amount of light collecting area – this would require many of the same changes as outlined above, but less growth in the stem would be necessary. Both of these solutions are limited by the plant's genetics.

Mathematics connections – Economy of GMOs

Days 9–10: Students reflect on their summaries for the contamination controversy, organize and share other reliable resources, and begin an Engineering Design Process to develop a protocol to reduce the likelihood of contamination of GMO seed into seed that is GMO free. This protocol will be the "rules" that all farmers use ensure that all GMO farmers use GMO seed and all non-GMO farmers use non-GMO seed.

The engineering design process is a series of steps that engineers follow when they are trying to solve a problem. The solution often involves designing a product (like a machine or a computer code) that needs to meet certain criteria and/or accomplish a particular task. In this case, the product is a set of standards that farmers must use to be sure they are doing as much as possible to keep GMO products (seed, food, and any tools that may have been used with GMO seed and food) away from non-GMO seed and food

The steps of the engineering process are:

- **Define:** Define the problem. What is the problem? How have others approached it? Identify the requirements.

- **Learn:** Brainstorm possible solutions and find the best solution.

- **Plan:** Do research, list materials needed, and identify steps you will take. Follow your plan and build a prototype.

- **Try**: Test the prototype. What works, what doesn't? What could you improve?

- **Decide:** Redesign to solve problems that came up in testing and retest.

- **Share:** Present it to others and let them give you feedback. After it has been critiqued, it often has to go back to the drawing table and be reconfigured and a new prototype is fashioned. Don't be discouraged if this happens. It is part of the process.

Students should be finding that the three sources of GMO contamination in organic farming:

1. Cross pollination (also sometimes known as pollen drift)

2. Human error in handling, harvesting, storage, and transportation

3. International trade methods for controlling contamination across borders have no protocol for testing GMO seeds or foods as they cross borders.

English Language Arts connections – Arguments

Day 10: Students should generate a written argument regarding what they think the most compelling arguments for and against GMOs in agriculture are based on two stakeholders that have opposing views.

Social Studies class – Ethics of GMOs

Day 10: Working in small groups and then as a class, have students form a plan for an approach that considers various stakeholders' views about GMOs in agriculture. Specifically, students should address how we can allow stakeholders that support GMOs to produce and access them while permitting stakeholders who oppose GMOs to avoid them. Any solution is feasible, but should balance both viewpoints. In particular, students should discuss the idea of labeling GMO products so that individuals can make their own decisions.

EVALUATE/ASSESSMENT

Performance Tasks – see attached rubrics for each of these tasks

1. Class participation rubric – Students will participate in whole class discussions, making claims that are backed up by evidence and reasoning.

2. Argument Graphic Organizer – Students will use the attached organizer to identify the components of arguments found in information resources

3. Student STEM research notebook – students will be keeping a research notebook with both entries regarding their experiment as well as answer to questions from webquests.

4. Cost-benefit analysis – Students will identify the appropriate inputs and outputs and conduct the cost-benefit analysis using appropriate mathematics skills.

Other Measures –

1. STEM research notebook entries- reviewed by the science teacher

INTERNET RESOURCES
Mathematics Resources

- http://thefoodiefarmer.blogspot.com/search?updated-min=2014-01-01T00:00:00-08:00&updated-max=2015-01-01T00:00:00-08:00&max-results=16.

English Language Arts Resources

- http://www.edutopia.org/blog/science-inquiry-claim-evidence-reasoning-eric-brunsell

- https://www.teachingchannel.org/videos/support-claims-with-evidence-getty

- https://www.youtube.com/watch?v=fkpZfpNWjWY

Social Studies Resources

- https://www.youtube.com/watch?v=YxFQ9MkwbDs.

Science Resources

- https://www.ck12.org/book/CK-12-Biology/section/16.2/

- http://grist.org/food/golden-apple-or-forbidden-fruit-following-the-money-on-gmos/

- http://www.aaas.org/news/statement-aaas-board-directors-labeling-genetically-modified-foods

- http://grist.org/food/are-gmos-worth-their-weight-in-gold-to-farmers-not-exactly/

- http://modernfarmer.com/2013/12/post-gmo-economy/

- http://www.ers.usda.gov/publications/err-economic-research-report/err162/report-summary.aspx

- http://www.isaaa.org/gmapprovaldatabase/default.asp

- http://www.bt.ucsd.edu/gmo.html

- https://en.wikipedia.org/wiki/Genetically_modified_crops

Class Participation Rubric

Students will participate in whole class discussions, making claims that are backed up by evidence and reasoning. A rubric for participation in the whole class discussion is found below:

Characteristic	Emerging (1)	Proficient (2)	Exemplary (3)
Follows guidelines of intellectual discussion and is civil	Criticizes other people personally instead of being critical of ideas; doesn't use appropriate language	Challenges the idea but without reason; uses appropriate language	Challenges the idea with solid reasoning; uses appropriate language; diverts any unproductive discussion
Makes claim	Claim unoriginal AND indirectly related to topic	Claim original AND indirectly related to topic	Claim original AND directly related to topic
Uses reliable sources for evidence	Uses unreliable resources (such as Wikipedia or blog)	Only uses textbook as resource	Uses outside reliable resources (such as a scientific journal or .gov or .edu website)
Appropriate level of evidence	Opinion-based evidence	One piece of researched evidence	More than one piece of researched evidence
Responds to the content of the discussion	No response or unrelated to claim	Response is indirectly associated with claim	Response is aligned with claim
Connects with what prior person says	Unrelated to current discussion	Stay on topic, but makes no connection with person before them	Acknowledges prior person's idea and elaborates on what previous person says
Able to defend their claim/rebuttal	Has no response	Has a response but cannot back up response	Has a response and is able to back up response with further evidence
Uses appropriate reasoning	Reasoning is disconnected from claim	Reasoning is superficially connected to claim	Reasoning directly connects claim to evidence

Argumentation Graphic Organizer

Problem/Question:

↓

Original Claim:

↓

Evidence	Reasoning
1.	
2.	
3.	

Evidence Number	Rebuttal	Valid	Rationale

STEM Research Notebook Rubric

	Beginning	Progressing	Advanced
Entries Related to Experimental Design			
Methods	Methods incomplete	Description of methods for planting seeds is clearly indicated BUT How each set of seeds were treated differently is not clear	Description of methods for planting seeds is clearly indicated AND How each set of seeds were treated differently within a particular experiment is clearly indicated
Raw Data	Daily data absent	Daily data present, but not easily found	Daily data are clearly indicated
Summarized Data	Data not organized in tables	Data organized in tables but no labels to indicate	Data organized in tables with clear labels for each column and row
Entries Related to Webquests			
Vocabulary	No vocabulary is used OR Vocabulary is not defined	Writing uses some vocabulary to convey the ideas OR Vocabulary isn't always defined	Writing effectively uses appropriate vocabulary to convey the ideas AND Vocabulary is defined
Use of facts and details	Few facts and details are provided	Facts and details chosen are not always appropriate for communicating ideas	Facts and details chosen are appropriate and effectively communicating the ideas
Use of examples	No examples are provided OR Examples do not communicate the ideas	Examples are provided to support ideas BUT Examples provided are too few OR Examples provided do not always effectively communicate the ideas	Examples are provided to support ideas AND All examples provided effectively communicate the ideas
Syntax	Uses poor sentence structure	Student mostly uses appropriate sentence structure	Student uses appropriate sentence structure
Overall Organization	Organization is lacking	Organization is apparent, but is not effective in building understanding of the topic	Organization effectively builds understanding of the topic
Answers Questions	Fewer than 3 questions are answered thoroughly	3 of the 4 questions are answered thoroughly	All questions are answered thoroughly

Cost/Benefit Rubric

	Beginning	Progressing	Advanced
Identifies appropriate inputs and outputs to compare	Students has included a few of the appropriate inputs that would be normal costs for farmers for both GMO and non-GMO's but may include inappropriate inputs OR Students have included some but not all of the relevant benefits for farmers for both GMO and non-GMO's – especially those that can be quantified but may also include inappropriate benefits	Students has included some but not all of the appropriate inputs that would be normal costs for farmers for both GMO and non-GMO's but does not include inappropriate inputs OR Students have included some but not all of the relevant benefits for farmers for both GMO and non-GMO's – especially those that can be quantified but does not include inappropriate benefits	Students has included all of the appropriate inputs that would be normal costs for farmers for both GMO and non-GMO's AND Students have included all of the relevant benefits for farmers for both GMO and non-GMO's – especially those that can be quantified.
Uses appropriate mathematics strategies to calculate overall costs and benefits	Inappropriate mathematics strategies are employed OR Most calculations are incorrect	Most mathematics strategies are appropriate OR Some calculation are incorrect	Mathematics strategies used are appropriate AND All calculations are correct
Conclusion from Cost/Benefit Analysis	Evaluation of the costs/benefits is limited; choices are based upon opinion and do not include the derived evidence from the cost/benefit analysis	Evaluation of the costs/benefits results in students choosing the option that with the ratio of cost/benefit in favor of the benefit side BUT Cannot explain how the cost/benefit analysis provided the evidence on which to base their claim	Evaluation of the costs/benefits results in students choosing the option that with the ratio of cost/benefit in favor of the benefit side AND Can explain how the cost/benefit analysis provided the evidence on which to base their claim

Lesson Plan 3: What Role Should The Government Play In GMOs?

LESSON SUMMARY

In this lesson, students will explore local, state, and national governments in relation to the GMO issue while continuing to examine data to describe how their plants are impacted by both the plants' genetics and the environment in which the plants are growing. In English Language Arts, students will examine plagiarism and the use of paraphrasing and quoting sources in communications.

ESSENTIAL QUESTION(S)
Science

- What effect do different levels of fertilizer have on plant growth?

Mathematics

- How do we summarize and communicate data for analysis?

English Language Arts

- How can we communicate information gained from resources without plagiarizing?

Social Studies

- What is the role of government (local, state, and federal) in addressing issues such as GMOs?

ESTABLISHED GOALS/OBJECTIVES
Science

- Students will be able to describe how the environment influences the growth and development of organisms.

Mathematics

- Students will be able to describe the role of descriptive statistics in summarizing data for communication and analysis.

- Students will be able to accurately calculate median, mean, range, and quartiles.

- Students will be able to explain the relationship between a research question and the type of graphs used to communicate and analyze data.

- Students will be able to effectively generate box-and-whiskers plots, bar graphs, and pie charts from data.

- Students will be able to interpret box-and-whiskers plots, bar graphs, and pie charts.

English Language Arts

- Students will be able to define plagiarism, paraphrasing, and quoting.

- Students will be able to create examples of plagiarism, paraphrasing, and the use of quotations.

- Students will explain why plagiarism is not appropriate.

- Students will explain how to paraphrase and use quotations effectively in a communication.

Social studies

- Students will be able to explain the relationship between legislation at the local, state, and federal levels.

TIME REQUIRED – 5 DAYS (45-MINUTE CLASS PERIODS)
NECESSARY MATERIALS
Science

- Days 11–12

  o Wisconsin Fast-Plants ™ or other plants that were planted during Lesson 1.
  o Tools for measuring – especially rulers and scales.

- Day 14

  o Data communications for Wisconsin Fast-Plants ™ data created by students at the end of math class (results showing descriptive statistics and box-and-whisker plots) for analysis and drawing conclusions.

Mathematics

- Day 11

  o Meter sticks or tape measures to measure the height of students.

o Some method of performing calculations such as a spreadsheet or calculator.

- Days 12–13

  o Communicating data to answer a research question (multiple parts)

- Day 14

  o Data collected in science class.
  o Some method of performing calculations such as a spreadsheet or calculator.

English Language Arts

- Days 11–12

  o Computers with Internet access for groups of students.
  o Plagiarism, paraphrasing, and quotations worksheets (attached at the end of this lesson).

- Days 13–15

  o Computers with Internet access for groups of students.

Social Studies

- Days 11–15

  o Computers with Internet access for groups of students.

Table 4.6. Standards Addressed in STEM Road Map Module Lesson Three

NEXT GENERATION SCIENCE STANDARDS
PERFORMANCE OBJECTIVES MS-LS1–3 – Use argument supported by evidence for how the body is a system of interacting subsystems composed of groups of cells. MS-LS1–5 – Construct a scientific explanation based on evidence for how environmental and genetic factors influence the growth of organisms.
DISCIPLINARY CORE IDEAS AND CROSSCUTTING CONCEPTS LS1.A: Structure and Function – In multicellular organisms, the body is a system of multiple interacting subsystems. These subsystems are groups of cells that work together to form tissues and organs that are specialized for particular body functions (MS-LS1-3) LS1.B: Growth and Development of Organisms – Organisms reproduce, either sexually or asexually, and transfer their genetic information to their offspring (secondary to MSLS3-2)

Continued

Genetically Modified Organisms, Grade 7

Table 4.6. (*continued*)

Science and Engineering Practices
ANALYZING AND INTERPRETING DATA – Analyzing data in 6–8 builds on K–5 experiences and progresses to extending quantitative analysis to investigations, distinguishing between correlation and causation, and basic statistical techniques of data and error analysis. Analyze displays of data to identify linear and nonlinear relationships. (MS-LS4-3); Analyze and interpret data to determine similarities and differences in findings. (MS-LS4-1)
USING mathematics AND COMPUTATIONAL THINKING – Mathematical and computational thinking in 6–8 builds on K–5 experiences and progresses to identifying patterns in large data sets and using mathematical concepts to support explanations and arguments. Use mathematical representations to support scientific conclusions and design solutions (MS-LS4-6)
CONSTRUCTING EXPLANATIONS AND DESIGNING SOLUTIONS – Constructing explanations and designing solutions in 6–8 builds on K–5 experiences and progresses to include constructing explanations and designing solutions supported by multiple sources of evidence consistent with scientific ideas, principles, and theories. Apply scientific ideas to construct an explanation for realworld phenomena, examples, or events. (MS-LS4–2); Construct an explanation that includes qualitative or quantitative relationships between variables that describe phenomena (MS-LS4-4)
OBTAINING, EVALUATING, AND COMMUNICATING INFORMATION – Obtaining, evaluating, and communicating information in 6–8 builds on K–5 experiences and progresses to evaluating the merit and validity of ideas and methods. Gather, read, and synthesize information from multiple appropriate sources and assess the credibility, accuracy, and possible bias of each publication and methods used, and describe how they are supported or not supported by evidence (MS-LS4-5)

COMMON CORE MATHEMATICS STANDARDS

MATHEMATICS CONTENT
7.NS.A.1 – Apply and extend previous understandings of addition and subtraction to add and subtract rational numbers; represent addition and subtraction on a horizontal or vertical number line diagram.
7.NS.A.3 – Solve real-world and mathematical problems involving the four operations with rational numbers (computations with rational numbers extend the rules for manipulating fractions to complex fractions).

COMMON CORE ENGLISH LANGUAGE ARTS STANDARDS

WRITING STANDARDS
W.7.1.A – Introduce claim(s), acknowledge alternate or opposing claims, and organize the reasons and evidence logically.
W.7.1.B – Support claim(s) with logical reasoning and relevant evidence, using accurate, credible sources and demonstrating an understanding of the topic or text.
W.7.1.C – Use words, phrases, and clauses to create cohesion and clarify the relationships among claim(s), reasons, and evidence.
W.7.1.E – Provide a concluding statement or section that follows from and supports the argument presented.

Table 4.6. (*continued*)

W.7.2.A – Introduce a topic clearly, previewing what is to follow; organize ideas, concepts, and information, using strategies such as definition, classification, comparison/contrast, and cause/effect; include formatting (e.g., headings), graphics (e.g., charts, tables), and multimedia when useful to aiding comprehension.

W.7.2.B – Develop the topic with relevant facts, definitions, concrete details, quotations, or other information and examples.

W.7.3 – Write narratives to develop real or imagined experiences or events using effective technique, relevant descriptive details, and well-structured event sequences.

W.7.6 – Use technology, including the Internet, to produce and publish writing and link to and cite sources as well as to interact and collaborate with others, including linking to and citing sources.

W.7.7 – Conduct short research projects to answer a question, drawing on several sources and generating additional related, focused questions for further research and investigation.

Reading Standards

RI.7.8 – Trace and evaluate the argument and specific claims in a text, assessing whether the reasoning is sound and the evidence is relevant and sufficient to support the claims.

RI.7.9 – Analyze how two or more authors writing about the same topic shape their presentations of key information by emphasizing different evidence or advancing different interpretations of facts.

21ST CENTURY SKILLS
Civic Literacy, Critical Thinking and Problem Solving

Table 4.7. Key Vocabulary for Lesson Three

Key Vocabulary	Definition
Box-and-whiskers plot	Type of graph that provides the central tendency, spread, and skewness of data
Descriptive statistics	Mathematical summaries of data that provide a particular description such as the central tendency of the data or the spread of the data
Paraphrasing	Summarizing information from a communication using your own words
Plagiarism	Knowingly or unknowingly using other ideas or products (including written communication) and claiming it as your own or failing to provide appropriate citations to the original work
Qualitative Data	Data that is a description of some feature of interest. It is not measured on a numerical scale (e.g., color, gender, etc.)
Quantitative Data	Data that is directly measured on a numerical scale (e.g., height, weight, etc.)
Quotations	Using others specific statements verbatim, but indicating that it is not your own words using quotation marks and citations appropriately

TEACHER BACKGROUND INFORMATION

Science

Students will begin drawing conclusions regarding the impact various fertilizer levels have on growth of their plants. It is important to help students understand that the fertilizer is not being directly used to perform photosynthesis but instead is necessary for creating the biomass that represents the growth process. Nitrogen, potassium, and phosphorous are used in making amino acids (for protein formation), nucleic acids, and lipids that provide the necessary building materials for new cells.

Mathematics

In this lesson, students will be focusing on describing data for use in communicating and analyzing data for a particular research question. The type of research question determines what types of descriptive statistics and graphical representations are appropriate. Students will be focusing on research questions regarding differences between at least two groups. Their data will likely be quantitative in nature; to examine their quantitative data, they will need to summarize the data using a measure of central tendency (mean and mode), spread of the data (range), and skewness (quartiles). Students can represent these numbers visually by creating box-and-whiskers plots. This type of graph shows all of the descriptive statistics at once and can allow students to compare multiple groups visually. If students are also looking at qualitative data, they will be able use percentages or counts as a means to communicate their results. This data can be communicated visually using bar graphs (for the count data it is appropriate as there is only one value) or pie/stacked-bar graphs (for percentage or count data as a proportion of the whole group).

English Language Arts

Students struggle with communicating ideas from other sources without plagiarizing. This lesson is intended to support them in developing the understanding of what plagiarism is, why it is inappropriate, and two methods to avoid it (paraphrasing and using quotations).

Social Studies

Understanding how local, state, and federal governmental legislation relate to one another is useful because there are current initiatives at the state level to require GMO labeling or banning GMO's altogether, while at the federal level there is legislation that would preempt any state or local authority to require or regulate GMO's. Having students understand how local, state, and federal laws are related will help them recognize that federal laws can supersede state and local laws. State laws can also supersede local laws.

LESSON PREPARATION

Science – See necessary materials

Mathematics – See necessary materials

English Language Arts – Need copies of the plagiarism, paraphrasing, and quotation worksheets for every student.

Safety Considerations

Students will be accessing information using the internet. Care should be taken to protect students from accessing internet sites that are inappropriate. Your IT contact person can provide guidance for appropriate search engines. Additionally, they may already have protective measures in place to prevent the students from accessing inappropriate content.

POTENTIAL MISCONCEPTIONS

Science

- Students may think that most of the biomass that that the plant produces is from the soil and not from the CO_2 and water.

Mathematics

- Student often think that any graph will work to communication and analysis.
- Students may think that the average and median are the same.

English Language Arts

- Students may think that using quotation marks around a statement is effectively communicating from other resources.

Social Studies

- Students may think that local, state, and federal laws always match and are on equal footing.

SAMPLE STRATEGIES FOR DIFFERENTIATION IN THIS MODULE

Science

- Product – All students will be evaluated on their conceptual understanding in their notebook. However, notebooks could be completed in digital format that

allows for images and audio recording. Students can use multiple methods to complete the argument to farmers activity.

Mathematics

- Content – Students can be focused on fewer descriptive stats.

- Process – Teachers can provide a more simplified worksheet for students to work through. Additionally, the worksheet provides the opportunity for more advanced students to work independently, while the teacher can focus more direct instruction on students that are struggling.

- Product – The worksheet can be modified to include more multiple-choice type questions.

English Language Arts

- Process – Providing a resources on plagiarism, paraphrasing and quotations can support students more. For struggling students, providing one or two focused resources may be provide even more support.

Social studies

- Process – Teachers may need to provide more or less direct instruction regarding how legislation at local, state and federal levels work depending on the students.

LEARNING PLAN COMPONENTS
INTRODUCTORY ACTIVITY/ENGAGEMENT
Science connections – Factors Influencing Growth

Day 11: Students should observe their plants. They should observe variation among the plants. Ask students why they think there is so much difference among the same species of plant. Students should conclude that it is likely that related plants were grown under different conditions. Tell students that they have actually set up three different sets of plants that they will use to explore what might cause these differences.

Mathematics connections – Communicating Data

Day 11: Ask students the following questions:

- How could we convey to the world what our class looks like?

- What if we wanted to compare this class with another class?

- What are ways that data can be communicated?

- Would we communicate the data exactly the same way for both purposes?

Discuss various features of students that could be used to describe the class. Have students focus on height of students (quantitative data) and eye color (qualitative data). Each student should record their height in centimeters and their eye color on the board. Students should then work in small groups to determine how they can go about communicating what the class looks like to their parents or the principal. This is a formative assessment to figure out what students know about descriptive statistics and graphing.

English Language Arts connections – How to Accurately Communicate Information From Sources

Day 11: Remind students that they will act as journalists when creating their documentary, and this will require they make statements that are both relevant and factual. Ask students where they will look for the information they are going to share. The students should recall that they gathered resources during the first lesson when they were trying to learn about the GMO issue. Discuss how students will use those resources in their documentary segments. Emphasize that as journalists students need to understand the following terms in order to use their resources effectively: plagiarism, quoting, and paraphrasing.

Social Studies class – Should the Government Regulate GMOs?

Day 11: Revisit the compromise the class determined the previous week. Ask students to consider whether all stakeholders will be satisfied. Are there some stakeholders that

may find this stance more of a concern? In particular remind students that the decision by the class is not binding in any way. Ask students to consider what can be done to get people to comply with the class' stance.

ACTIVITY/INVESTIGATION

Science connections – Factors Influencing Growth

Day 11: Ask the question: What kinds of measurements would we want to use to determine if any factors influenced the growth of our plant? Students should generate a list that includes qualitative and quantitative data. Have the students focus attention on data that would indicate that the plant's overall function is impacted positively or negatively. Any of the following would be good examples:

- Leaf size – influences how much light can be captured

- Amount of green in leaf – reflects the amount of chlorophyll and photosynthesis that can happen

- Plant height – is a measure of how much growth is occurring

- Stem thickness – describes how much support the plant has as it grows upward

- Photosynthetic rate – measures production of food directly

- Root depth – influences how much support for growing taller there is

- Root mass – influences both support and water function.

After generating the list, lead a discussion to encourage students to recognize that some of the data they are describing is quantifiable (can be expressed mathematically) and others are differences of quality (cannot be defined in mathematical terms). Work with students to understand the difference and the role of each type of data. Have students work in their groups to determine 1–2 variables they will focus on for their investigations (note: plant height and leaf size are two good ones on which to focus).

Day 12: In groups, students will be assigned a group of plants from one of the three investigations to measure and record data (the students should have decided which variable they will be measuring on Day 11 – see list of possible variables students might identify). Lead a discussion about data tables, accurate and consistent recording of measurements, and the use of metric measurements. The data should be compiled to share with the class.

Mathematics connections – Communicating Data

Days 11–13: Provide the class with the "Communicating Data to Answer a Research Question" worksheet starting with Part 1. Provide additional parts as the class proceeds. At the end of each part, lead a discussion with the class about what they have learned (see teacher comments in the worksheet).

English Language Arts connections – How to Accurately Communicate Information From Sources

Days 11–12: Students will be doing research using a jigsaw learning method to learn about plagiarism, paraphrasing, and quotations. This is done by first having students working in expert groups in which they will learn and figure about a particular topic and consider out how to communicate their knowledge. For this part of the jigsaw method, split students into three expert groups focusing on either plagiarism, paraphrasing, or quotations. They will work in these groups to conduct a webquest to answer the questions on the specific section of the worksheet their group was assigned.

Social Studies class – Should the Government Regulate GMOs?

Days 11–14: Students should explore the news to understand the current governmental response to GMO crops in food (local, state, and national level). During this review, they should focus on the following questions:

Local Governments:

- What are some examples of how local governments are trying to regulate GMOs?

- What is the reason these governments have decided that regulation is necessary?

State Governments:

- What are some examples of how state governments are trying to regulate GMOs?

- What is the reason these governments have decided that regulation is necessary?

National Government:

- How is the U.S. Government responding to GMO regulation?

- What is the reason the U.S. Government has taken these actions?

Examples of articles from regarding GMO labeling required at the local, state, and national level can be found below. Additionally, these articles can lead to the original bills that were introduced (three are listed below).

- https://protecttheharvest.com/news/saying-no-to-gmos-municipal-government-bans-on-genetically-modified-foods/ – this article has examples of municipal ordinances that are requiring labeling or banning GMOs.

- http://ecowatch.com/2014/03/08/gmos-ban-them-or-label-them/ – this is a good overview article of the local, state, national and international legislation on GMOs.

- http://www.kansascity.com/news/government-politics/article28423006. html – article focusing on the Safe and Accurate Food Labeling Act and its implications.

- http://www.statesmanjournal.com/story/tech/science/ environment/2015/07/15/congress-moving-ban-state-local-gmo-regulation/30217703/ – article describing the Safe and Accurate Food Labeling Act and its implications to the municipal ordinances.

- https://www.congress.gov/bill/114th-congress/house-bill/1599/text -Safe and Accurate Food Labeling Act Bill

- https://ballotpedia.org/California_Proposition_37,_Mandatory_Labeling_of_ Genetically_Engineered_Food_(2012)

- https://ballotpedia.org/Washington_Mandatory_Labeling_of_Genetically_ Engineered_Food_Measure,_Initiative_522_(2013)

EXPLAIN

Science connections – Factors Influencing Growth

Days 14–15: The students will work in teams to draw conclusions regarding how the varying fertilizer conditions influenced the plant focusing on variables assigned by the teacher. Students should be given variables that show variations and others that do not show variation. Using what they know about plant structure and function, students should discuss how any differences found would impact the overall function of the plant. This should be completed as a written entry in students' STEM research notebooks.

Mathematics connections – Communicating Data

Days 11–13: Discuss the use of descriptive statistics and graphs to answer research questions containing quantitative and qualitative data. See worksheet for specific comments.

English Language Arts connections – How to Accurately Communicate Information From Sources

Day 12: To continue the investigation using the jigsaw method (see Day 11), students will move from their expert groups into their home groups. Each home group will have one person each who completed the plagiarizing, paraphrasing, and quotation section of the worksheet. Each student will share the portion of the worksheet he/she completed with the group, teaching the other students about the term and its importance in communicating ideas and information.

As a class, guide students to develop a set of guidelines they will use for communication in their documentary. Students' guidelines should demonstrate an understanding of what plagiarism is, an understanding of the correct and judicious use of quotations, and an understanding of the importance of paraphrasing accurately.

Social Studies class – Should the Government Regulate GMOs?

Day 15: Lead a discussion regarding how the local, state, and federal governments are responding to concerns about GMOs. During this discussion, explain to students how legislation at the local, state, and federal government levels relate to one another. Focus the students on the concept that local ordinances can be pre-empted by state or federal laws and that state laws can be pre-empted by federal laws

EXTEND/APPLY KNOWLEDGE

Science connections – Factors Influencing Growth

Day 15: Discuss with the class the importance of plant reproduction in agriculture and how the growth rate of plants is often a good indicator of productivity. If a plant can easily get the nutrients it needs, it can put its energy into generating the fruits and vegetables we eat.

Give the following as a homework assignment:

Write a summary of what you learned about plant fertilizer and how you could use this knowledge to increase plant growth and productivity. What would you recommend to farmers regarding using fertilizer? Why? Focus on providing a recommendation (claim), evidence (interpretation of the data summary), and reasoning (why this recommendations would work; i.e., the science behind the recommendation).

Mathematics connections – Communicating Data

Day 13: Introduce the lesson by pointing out that student have collected a number of measurements about their plants in the three investigations. Ask students how they can communicate this information. Students should explain what descriptive statistics and which graphs they could use for each of the three investigations. Divide students into groups and create the data communication (results) for one of the three investigations. Each group should then share their data communication with the class.

English Language Arts connections – How to Accurately Communicate Information From Sources

Days 12–15: Students will begin organizing a written communication focusing on answers to the following questions:

- What is a GMO? How are they created?

- What are examples of GMOs that currently exist?

- Who stands to profit or lose with the production and sale of GMOs? (who are the stakeholders?)

- What are possible benefits from GMOs in agriculture?

- What are possible threats from GMOs in agriculture?

Social Studies class

N/A

EVALUATE/ASSESSMENT

Performance Tasks – See Attached Rubrics

1. Class participation rubric – Students will participate in whole class discussions, making claims that are backed up by evidence and reasoning.

2. Data communication of investigations – students will choose appropriate descriptive statistics and visual representations of the data (tabular or graphical) based on the research question for a particular investigation.

3. Recommendations to farmers – students will use their data to argue a particular recommendation to farmers to improve their plant growth and potential productivity.

Other Measures

1. Plagiarizing, paraphrasing, quotation worksheet – see attached

2. English Language Arts Teacher examination of the developing communication

INTERNET RESOURCES

- http://protecttheharvest.com/2015/06/23/saying-no-to-gmos-municipal-government-bans-on-genetically-modified-foods/ – this article has examples of municipal ordinances that are requiring labeling or banning GMO's.

- http://ecowatch.com/2014/03/08/gmos-ban-them-or-label-them/ – this is a good overview article of the local, state, national and international legislation on GMO's.

- http://www.kansascity.com/news/government-politics/article28423006.html – article focusing on the Safe and Accurate Food Labeling Act and its implications.

- http://www.statesmanjournal.com/story/tech/science/environment/2015/07/15/congress-moving-ban-state-local-gmo-regulation/

30217703/ – article describing the Safe and Accurate Food Labeling Act and its implications to the municipal ordinances.

- https://www.congress.gov/bill/114th-congress/house-bill/1599/text -Safe and Accurate Food Labeling Act Bill

- https://ballotpedia.org/California_Proposition_37,_Mandatory_Labeling_of_Genetically_Engineered_Food_(2012)

- https://ballotpedia.org/Washington_Mandatory_Labeling_of_Genetically_Engineered_Food_Measure,_Initiative_522_(2013)

PART 1 – HOW CAN WE COMMUNICATE QUANTITATIVE DATA TO ANSWER A RESEARCH QUESTION?

The worksheet that follows contains the teacher version of the worksheet. Comments and answers are found in italics.

Scientists have been studying plants found at different locations on a mountain in a nearby nature preserve. They have already identified several study sites at different elevations (heights) up on the mountain. They have a total of 72 sites on the mountain where they have been studying the plants. They are especially interested in determining if temperature influences the plant species. They know that sites closer to the bottom of the mountain would be warmer than sites closer to the top of the mountain. For their study that selected 24 sites at a low elevation (0 m – at the base of the mountain), 24 sites at a middle elevation (500 m above the base of the mountain) and 24 sites at a high elevation (1000 m above the base of the mountain).

To make sure there were temperature differences at these elevations before they started their project, they collected temperature measurements at the same time (same day, same time of day, etc.). Table 4.8 shows the data they collected.

1. What is their research question? ***Does the temperature at different elevations differ?***

2. What would you do to help them use their data to try and answer the question? Explain why you would do that.

Answers will vary here based on the students' experiences. Lead a discussion with students about what they would do and why before you move to part 2.

Table 4.8. Temperature (°C) for each site at each elevation

High (1000 m)	Mid (500 m)	Low (0 m)
15.2	15.8	16.8
14.8	15.2	16.8
14.7	15.2	16.4
14.54	14.8	16.2
14.5	14.7	15.6
14.49	14.7	15.5
14.46	14.7	15.4
14.43	14.6	15.3
14.4	14.6	15.2
14.38	14.5	14.9
14.36	14.4	14.9
14.35	14.3	14.8
14.3	14.3	14.8
14.23	14.1	14.8
14.2	14	14.6
14.16	13.9	14.5
14.13	13.9	14.5
14.1	13.9	14.5
13.7	13.9	14.5
13.8	13.9	14.4
13.7	13.8	14.4
13.5	13.7	14.2
13.4	13.6	14.2
12.7	13.5	13.9

If students suggest taking an average or other descriptive stats, discuss with them that average is a calculated description of the data that can be easily communicated and compared. Discuss with the students that this is called a descriptive statistic. Ask them if they know of other descriptive statistics that can be used to describe the data.

If students suggest graphing the data, ask why graphs might be useful. Have them highlight that it is a visual way to describe the data in a way that patterns can be seen or compared.

Once they have exhausted their ideas move on to part 2: What does the Box-and-Whiskers Plot Tell Us about a Collection of Data.

PART 2 WHAT DOES THE BOX-AND-WHISKERS PLOT TELL US ABOUT A COLLECTION OF DATA?

The scientists first focused on describing the temperature data for the high elevation sites. They created the graph found in Figure 4.1, using the table of data found to the right.

1. Draw a line for the value in the table that matches the top of the line that runs up and down. What is that value? *15.2*

2. Draw a line for the value in the table that matches the bottom of the lines that runs up and down through the box. What is that value? *12.7*

3. What does the center line in the Box-and-Whisker tell you about the data? *It describes the minimum and maximum of the dataset. This represents the range of all the data*

4. What is the estimated value of the line separating the grey and orange box? Draw a line from the value on the graph to where it would possibly be in the table (if it is between two values, end the line between the two values) *Around 14.33*

5. Looking at the table, how many data points are above and below the value you found in number 4? What percentage of all the points is that? *There are 12 points which is roughly half*

6. The value you found in part four is called the median. Based on what you have seen with the data, how would you define the term median? (hint: where does it fall in terms of all of the data?) *It is the middle of the ordered data. When clarifying with the students, make sure they understand that this is an example of a central tendency of the data (like average/mean would be)*

7. What is the estimated value at the bottom of the orange box? Draw a line from the value on the graph to where it would possibly be in the table (if it is between two values, end the line between the two values) *Around 14.25*

8. How many data points are between the bottom of the orange box and the median? What percentage of the data is represented in this area? *There are 6 data points which is 25%*

9. How many data points are below the bottom of the orange box? What percentage of the data is represented in this area? *There are 6 data points which is 25%*

10. This range below the bottom of the orange box is called the 1st quartile. The range between the bottom of the orange box and the median is called the 2nd quartile. Based on this information, how would you define a quartile? *A quarter of the data*

11. Label the 1st and 2nd quartile on the graph

12. What is the estimated value at the top of the grey box? Draw a line from the value on the graph to where it would possibly be in the table (if it is between two values, end the line between the two values) *Around 14.6*

13. Based on what you have already learned about quartiles, label where you think the 3rd and 4th quartiles are located on the graph.

14. On a Box-and-Whiskers plot, what does the top and bottom boxes represent? *The quartiles or 25% of the data directly above and below the median*

15. Why are the grey and orange box not the same size? *Data in the 2nd quartile have a much wider range than the data in the 3rd quartile*

Figure 4.1. Box-and-Whiskers Plot for the research question: Describe the temperature across the sites. The graph shows the summarized data information for 24 high elevation sites. Notice the scale on the y-axis does not start at zero. This was done to allow a more detailed view of the plot

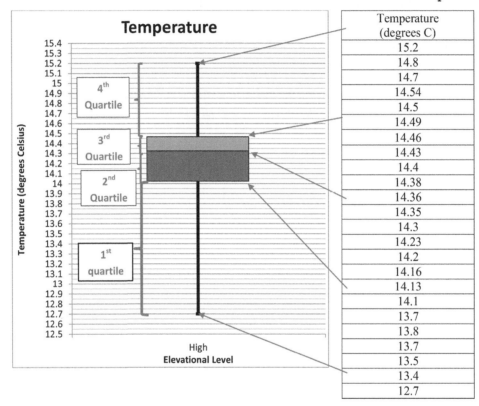

PART 3 – HOW CAN WE COMMUNICATE OUR TEMPERATURE DATA EFFECTIVELY?

There are lots of different kinds of graphs that are available for graphing data, but the scientists chose the Box-and-Whiskers plot over others. Why? The purpose of graphs is to communicate as much information about the data as possible. When the research question is focused on describing the data of one group or comparing data among multiple groups, scientists like to have some way to describe the following three aspects of the data:

- The middle of the data (central tendency) – Since all of the data points aren't exactly the same, the middle of data is likely to be value that could represent all values. The middle of the data described in the Box-and-Whiskers plot in part 2 was the median. Average is also an example of the central tendency. This can also be thought of as the balance point of the data as the values should be relatively equally spread on either side of the middle.

- The spread of the data – Describing how spread out the data is gives some indication of how much variation there is in the data. The more spread out, the more the data is different among the samples. The less spread out, the more closely the data is among the samples. In the Box-and-Whiskers plot, the spread of the data was described by the range.

- Where most of the data lies across the spread (sometime known as skew) – Knowing how the data points are distributed along the spread provides information about how to interpret the other 2 parts (central tendency and spread). In the Box-and-Whiskers plot, the skew of the data was described by the quartiles (size of the boxes and length of range line on either side of the median).

By using these three aspects, the scientists can effectively communicate all of the information in the data and look for patterns.

Could the scientists have used any graphs to show the three aspects described above? Take a look at part Figure 4.2. It shows three graphs using the same data for high elevations.

1. Figure 4.2a is a bar graph of every data point in the table. So every sample taken at 1000 m is given its own bar on the graph.

    a. Can you identify a specific central tendency? If yes, what is that value? **Not really, it would have to be estimated**

    b. Can you identify the range? If yes, what is that value? **Around 12.7 to 15.2**

    c. Can you identify where most of the data lies across the spread? If yes, what is that value? **Not really, it would have to be estimated**

Figure 4.2a. These graphs are created from the same data table used in Figure 4.1

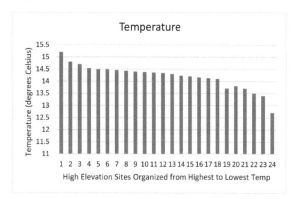

Figure 4.2c. These graphs are created from the same data table used in Figure 4.1

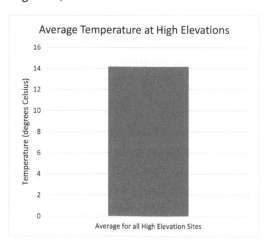

Figure 4.2b. These graphs are created from the same data table used in Figure 4.1

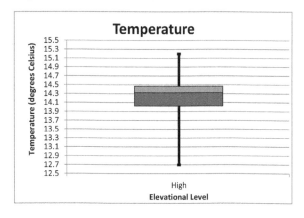

2. Figure 4.2b is the same Box-and-Whiskers plot seen in part 2.

    a. Can you identify a specific central tendency? If yes, what is that value?
        About 14.3
    b. Can you identify the range? If yes, what is that value? ***Around 12.7 to 15.2***
    c. Can you identify where most of the data lies across the spread? If yes, what
        is that value? ***The data tends to fall across a wider spread below the median
        compared to the top***

3. Figure 4.2c is a bar graph of the average of all of the data for 1000 m.

   a. Can you identify a specific central tendency? If yes, what is that value?
   Around 14.2

   b. Can you identify the range? If yes, what is that value? **No, it is not available**

   c. Can you identify where most of the data lies across the spread? If yes, what is that value? **No, it is not available**

4. Based on what you see above, which of the three graphs most <u>effectively</u> communicate the three major aspects of the data that scientists like to describe? **Box-and-Whiskers plot**

Discussing these results with the students will be very helpful. You may also wish to present other types of graphs (line graph, stacked bar graph) and discuss whether these would describe all three aspects of the data. Reinforce that these aspects are primarily important because the research question is focused on describing the data for one group or comparing groups.

PART 4 – COMPARING TEMPERATURES AT DIFFERENT ELEVATIONS?

The scientists weren't satisfied with just showing the data for the high elevation sites because it did not help them answer their research question. What they wanted to do was to also look at the data for the other two sites and compare them.

1. Use the data in table 4.9 to create Box-and-Whiskers plots for all three elevations. **Students should get a figure that looks like below.**

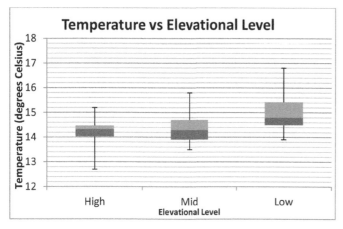

2. What does this data same about the temperatures at each of these elevations? **Students should explain that the higher and mid-elevations have lower temperatures compared the low. There really doesn't seem to be a difference between the median temperature of the high and mid elevations. However, most of the data (skew) falls over a lower range than does the mid elevations. Other descriptions are also possible regarding the size of the quartiles, etc.**

Table 4.9. Temperature (°C) for each site at each elevation

High (1000 m)	Mid (500 m)	Low (0 m)
15.2	15.8	16.8
14.8	15.2	16.8
14.7	15.2	16.4
14.54	14.8	16.2
14.5	14.7	15.6
14.49	14.7	15.5
14.46	14.7	15.4
14.43	14.6	15.3
14.4	14.6	15.2
14.38	14.5	14.9
14.36	14.4	14.9
14.35	14.3	14.8
14.3	14.3	14.8
14.23	14.1	14.8
14.2	14	14.6
14.16	13.9	14.5
14.13	13.9	14.5
14.1	13.9	14.5
13.7	13.9	14.5
13.8	13.9	14.4
13.7	13.8	14.4
13.5	13.7	14.2
13.4	13.6	14.2
12.7	13.5	13.9

PART 5 – HOW DO WE COMMUNICATE DATA TO ANSWER A RESEARCH QUESTION?

The scientists wanted to describe the type of tree species they were finding in at the different elevations on the mountain. Their research question was what were the species of tree present, how many of each species, and in what proportions for each elevation. What they found was that there were only 5 different tree species in their study areas with different numbers of individuals for each species at each elevation. Table 4.10 shows their data.

Table 4.10. Number of individuals of different species at different elevations

	High Elevations	Mid Elevations	Low Elevations
Species 1	15	30	63
Species 2	10	30	52
Species 3	40	25	9
Species 4	5	10	12
Species 5	20	25	40

1. Is the data they have quantitative or qualitative? ***Students might argue that the data is quantitative since there are numbers of individuals in each species. Remind the students that an individual can only be classified as one of five species. Therefore, the data the scientists are collecting is qualitative. The count of the individuals in each category is one way to communicate information about qualitative data.***

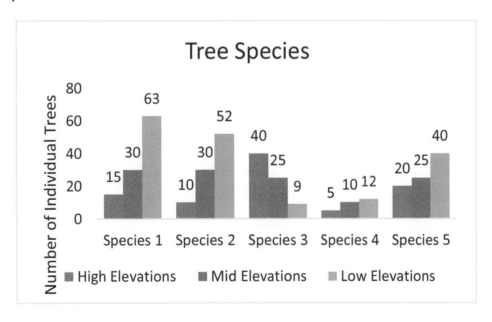

2. Look at the count data data in Table 4.10 and answer the following: ***After looking at these questions, the students should recognize that count data of qualitative characters cannot be described using the same properties as quantitative data.***

    a. Is there a central tendency? ***no***
    b. Is there a spread? ***no***
    c. Can you identify where most of the data lies across the spread? ***no***

3. Currently, the scientists have counted all of the individuals in their sites. If you look at their research questions, one part is to get a count of all the individuals in each species. They could stick with this data table to communicate the answer and this would be just fine. However, it doesn't make for easy comparison of the different sites. They would also like to communicate it graphically. Which of the graphs have we explored so far do you think would communicate count data effectively? Create that graph using the table data above. ***Students might try to use a variety of graph types. After they have shared the graphs, students should be guided to a bar or column graph would be appropriate for communicating count data as it communicates one value per category and the data collected only has one value per category. See graph to left as example.***

PART 6 – HOW DO WE COMMUNICATE DATA TO ANSWER A RESEARCH QUESTION? PROPORTIONS

1. The scientists had a third question regarding the proportions of the 5 different species they have at each elevation. How do we go about getting a proportion? *Students should explore their options and then be guided to calculating a percentage. In particular, they should understand that a percentage is what part of the whole a sample would represent.*

2. What would the proportions of each species be at different elevation? Create a table to show these values.

Table 4.11. Percentage of individuals of different species at different elevations

	High Elevations	Mid Elevations	Low Elevations
Species 1	17%	25%	36%
Species 2	11%	25%	30%
Species 3	44%	21%	5%
Species 4	6%	8%	7%
Species 5	22%	21%	23%

3. How does this new calculation allow us to make a comparisons across the elevations? *We can now look for changes in proportion of individuals. For instance, species 4 and 5 do not seem to change with elevation but species 1–3 really change with elevation.*

4. What were the total values of individuals found at each elevation? Do they differ? *90 at high, 120 at mid, 176 at low – the low elevation has twice as many individuals at at the high elevations.*

5. Knowing the total value of the individuals used for calculating a percentage is also useful. If you had the total number of individuals found at each elevation, could you figure out how many actual individuals were present in the sample? How? *Yes, by the following equation total*%=number of individuals. This is a good place to discuss with students that having more information is better than less as it communicates more information for analysis.*

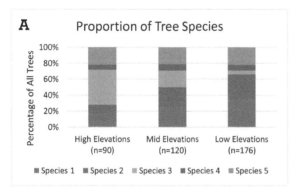

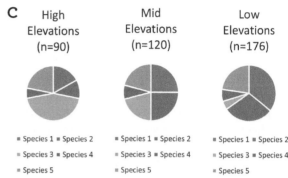

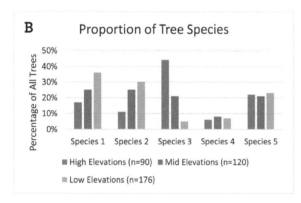

Figure 4.3. Graphs showing proportions of species at different elevations. Proportions derived from data found in table 4.10. Graph A is a stacked bar graph showing species proportions at each elevation. Graph B is a bar graph showing the proportion at each elevation grouped by species. Graph C are pie graphs showing proportions of each species at each elevation

6. If we wanted to graphically communicate the proportions, what type of graphs would we use? Figure 4.3 provides 3 examples of graphs of the proportions.

   a. What does the letter n stand for in the graphs? ***Students should be able to state that this is the total number of individuals.***

   b. Why do we report the n in the graph? ***To provide as much information about the data as possible.***

   c. Which of the graphs are effective for visually comparing the proportions at each elevation? ***Students should notice they all provide the same information but that figures A and C are more effective for comparing proportions as they show the percentages in a way that can be easily compared.***

7. Why would a box-and-whiskers plot not be appropriate for this type of data? ***There is only one value for each species. Median, range, and skew do not apply to this kind of data.***

8. Using one of the graphs you identified in Figure 4.3, discuss how the tree species compare at the different elevations. ***Students should be able to say that at higher elevations, there tend to be fewer trees. Additionally, species 4 and 5 tend to be present in about the same proportions regardless of elevation. Species 3 is more common at higher elevations while species 1 and 2 are more common at lower elevations.***

PART 6 – APPLYING YOUR KNOWLEDGE?

The class collected data to answer the research questions:

- What does the height of our class look like?

- What does the eye color of our class look like?

Communicate the data to answer these questions and provide answer. Use the Parts 1–5 to reflect on ways you can effectively communicate your data.

Students should choose a box and whiskers plot of their height data and either stacked bar or pie graph for the eye color data.

Class Participation

Students will participate in whole class discussions, making claims that are backed up by evidence and reasoning. A rubric for participation in the whole class discussion is found below:

Characteristic	Emerging (1)	Proficient (2)	Exemplary (3)
Follows guidelines of intellectual discussion and is civil	Criticizes other people personally instead of being critical of ideas; doesn't use appropriate language	Challenges the idea but without reason; uses appropriate language	Challenges the idea with solid reasoning; uses appropriate language; diverts any unproductive discussion
Makes claim	Claim unoriginal AND indirectly related to topic	Claim original AND indirectly related to topic	Claim original AND directly related to topic
Uses reliable sources for evidence	Uses unreliable resources (such as Wikipedia or blog)	Only uses textbook as resource	Uses outside reliable resources (such as a scientific journal or .gov or .edu website)
Appropriate level of evidence	Opinion-based evidence	One piece of researched evidence	More than one piece of researched evidence
Responds to the content of the discussion	No response or unrelated to claim	Response is indirectly associated with claim	Response is aligned with claim
Connects with what prior person says	Unrelated to current discussion	Stay on topic, but makes no connection with person before them	Acknowledges prior person's idea and elaborates on what previous person says
Able to defend their claim/rebuttal	Has no response	Has a response but cannot back up response	Has a response and is able to back up response with further evidence
Uses appropriate reasoning	Reasoning is disconnected from claim	Reasoning is superficially connected to claim	Reasoning directly connects claim to evidence

Plagiarism, Paraphrasing, and Quotations Worksheet
Plagiarism

What is plagiarism?

Where did you find that definition?

Did you plagiarize that definition? How would you know?

Why is plagiarism a problem?

Create two examples of plagiarism that would show someone how they could tell if they are plagiarizing. Provide the passage that is plagiarized and a written communication that is plagiarizing that passage.

EXAMPLE 1:

Passage plagiarized:

Communication that has plagiarized the passage:

EXAMPLE 2:

Passage plagiarized:

Communication that has plagiarized the passage:

Paraphrasing

What is paraphrasing?

Where did you find that definition?

Did you paraphrase that definition? How would you know?

Why is paraphrasing a good thing when communicating material found in other people's work?

Create two examples of paraphrasing that would show someone how they could take information and paraphrase it. Provide the passage that is paraphrased and a written communication that is paraphrasing that passage.
EXAMPLE 1:
Passage paraphrased:

Communication that has paraphrased the passage:

EXAMPLE 2:
Passage paraphrased:

Communication that has paraphrased the passage:

Quotations

What is a quotation?

Where did you find that definition?

Did you quote the definition? How would you know?

When would quotations be a useful?

Should you use quotations a lot in your communications? Why or why not?

Create two examples of using quotations that would show someone how they could do it correctly. Provide the passage that is being quoted from and a written communication that is quoting from that passage.

EXAMPLE 1:

Passage quoted from:

Communication that has quote from the passage:

EXAMPLE 2:

Passage quoted from:

Communication that has quote from the passage:

Rubric for Data Communication

	Beginning	Progressing	Advanced
Central Tendency of Quantitative Data	Cannot explain what the mean and median describe about the data and when they are appropriate to use AND Does not use appropriate mathematic procedures to determine the mean and median for a set of data	Explain what the mean and median describe about the data and when they are appropriate to use OR Can use appropriate mathematic procedures to determine the mean and median for a set of data	Explain what the mean and median describe about the data and when they are appropriate to use AND Can use appropriate mathematic procedures to determine the mean and median for a set of data
Spread of Quantitative Data	Cannot explain what the range describe about the data and when it is appropriate to use AND Does not use appropriate mathematic procedures to determine the range for a set of data	Explain what the range describe about the data and when it is appropriate to use OR Can use appropriate mathematic procedures to determine the range for a set of data	Explain what the range describes about the data and when it is appropriate to use AND Can use appropriate mathematic procedures to determine the range for a set of data
Skewness of Quantitative Data	Cannot explain what the quartiles describe about the data and when they are appropriate to use AND Does not use appropriate mathematic procedures to determine the quartiles for a set of data	Explain what the quartiles describe about the data and when they are appropriate to use OR Can use appropriate mathematic procedures to determine the quartiles for a set of data	Explain what the quartiles describe about the data and when they are appropriate to use AND Can use appropriate mathematic procedures to determine the quartiles for a set of data
Box-and-Whiskers Plot for Quantitative Data	Cannot explain the use of a box-and-whiskers plot AND Cannot correctly construct a box-and-whiskers plot with appropriate labels and descriptions	Explain the use of a box-and-whiskers plot AND Correctly construct a box-and-whiskers plot that has some appropriate labels and descriptions	Explain the use of a box-and-whiskers plot AND Correctly construct a box-and-whiskers plot with appropriate labels and descriptions

Continued

Rubric for Data Communication (*continued*)

	Beginning	Progressing	Advanced
Percentages Describing Qualitative Data	Cannot explain what percentages describe about the data and when they are appropriate to use AND Does not use appropriate mathematic procedures to determine the percentages for a set of data	Explain what percentages describe about the data and when they are appropriate to use OR Can use appropriate mathematic procedures to determine the percentages for a set of data	Explain what percentages describe about the data and when they are appropriate to use AND Can use appropriate mathematic procedures to determine the percentages for a set of data
Bar Graph for Qualitative Data	Cannot explain the use of a bar graph OR Construct a bar graph without appropriate labels and descriptions	Explain the use of a bar graph OR Correctly construct a bar graph with appropriate labels and descriptions	Explain the use of a bar graph AND Correctly construct a bar graph with appropriate labels and descriptions

Rubric for Recommendations to Farmers Using Data

	Beginning	Progressing	Advanced
Makes a recommendation	Recommendation is not related to the topic	Recommendation is directly related to topic BUT Does not seem reasonable given the evidence	Recommendation is directly related to topic AND Is reasonable given the evidence
Uses evidence to support recommendation	Does not provide evidence in the data communication to support the evidence	Interprets the data communication correctly BUT Does not relate the evidence in the data communication to support the evidence	Interprets the data communication correctly AND Relates the evidence in the data communication to support the evidence
Reasoning	Reasoning does not discuss the impact that fertilizer has on growth	Reasoning discusses the impact that fertilizer has on growth and development BUT Does not show understanding of the role fertilizer has in growth	Reasoning explains of how fertilizer impacts growth, showing and understanding of the role that fertilizer has on growth

Rubric for Developing GMO Communication

	Beginning	Progressing	Advanced
Appropriate use of paraphrasing and quotations	Plagiarizes material OR Students over-reliant on using quotations	Students use some paraphrasing and judicious use of quotes	Students effectively use paraphrasing and judicious use of quotes in their developing communication
Examples of Paraphrasing	Few examples of paraphrasing are good	Some examples of paraphrasing are good	All examples of paraphrasing are good
Examples of quotes usage	Few examples of using quotes are correctly done	Some examples of using quotes are correctly done	All examples of using quotes are correctly done

Lesson Plan 4: Does The Media Influence Our Perspectives?

LESSON SUMMARY

Students will focus on their documentary in this lesson. Each class will create its own documentary in segments focusing on different aspects of the GMO issue. Student groups will be assigned as the lead creators of different segments when they begin the documentary production.

- Introduction – 5 min – Created by the teacher with assistance from the kids.

- Segment 1–10 min

  o What is a GMO? How are they created?
  o What are examples of GMO that current exist?
  o How have organisms' genetic makeups been altered in the past?

- Segment 2–10 min

  o What are possible benefits from GMOs in agriculture?

- Segment 3–10 min

  o What are possible threats from GMOs in agriculture?

- Segment 4–10 min

  o Who are the stakeholders and what are their stances?

- Segment 5–10 min

  o What is the government at the local, state, and federal levels doing to address the concerns of stakeholders?

In social studies they will explore how the Internet and media influence the amount and quality of information available to citizens as compared to the pre-Internet era. In English Language Arts, students will be given their assignments for their portion of the overall documentary and will discuss the plan for creating the documentary. In science, students will complete their exploration of how the genes and environment influence the growth of organisms. They will also explore how humans have used selective breeding to influence genes of organisms to our benefit.

ESSENTIAL QUESTION(S)
Science

- How do genes influence the growth of organisms?

- What technologies have humans used to influence the inheritance of desired traits in organisms?

English Language Arts

- How do we make a documentary?

Social Studies

- How has the Internet influenced the way that people find information about issues compared to the past?

- How has the Internet influenced the way issues are explored and discussed?

ESTABLISHED GOALS/OBJECTIVES
Science

- Students will be able to explain how variations in a gene can result in different traits in an organism.

- Students will be able to describe how humans have influenced the inheritance of desired traits in organisms through selective breeding.

English Language Arts

- Students will identify the most important information they need to convey for their portion of the documentary.

- Students will describe how they will engage their viewers as well as close their section in a way that makes their section a unified whole.

- Students will create interview questions that will elicit specific types of responses from those being interviewed.

Social Studies

- Students will be able to explain how information literacy has changed in the past 40 years.

- Students will examine why GMOs are an issue while selective breeding in agriculture is not.

TIME REQUIRED – 5 DAYS (45-MINUTE CLASS PERIODS)
NECESSARY MATERIALS
Science

- Days 21–22

  o Plants that were planted during Lesson 1.
  o Tools for measuring – especially rulers and scales.

o Data communications (results showing descriptive statistics and box-and-whisker plots) for analysis and drawing conclusions.

• Days 23–25

o Computers with Internet access for groups of students.

English Language Arts

• Days 21–25

o Computers with Internet access for groups of students.
o Video cameras.
o Video editing software.

Social Studies

• Days 21–25

o Computers with Internet access for groups of students.

Table 4.12. Standards Addressed in STEM Road Map Module Lesson Four

---

NEXT GENERATION SCIENCE STANDARDS

PERFORMANCE OBJECTIVES

MS-LS1–5 – Construct a scientific explanation based on evidence for how environmental and genetic factors influence the growth of organisms.

MS-LS4–5 – Gather and synthesize information about the technologies that have changed the way humans in-fluence the inheritance of desired traits in organisms.

DISCIPLINARY CORE IDEAS AND CROSSCUTTING CONCEPTS

LS3.A: Inheritance of Traits – Genes are located in the chromosomes of cells, with each chromosome pair containing two variants of each of many distinct genes. Each distinct gene chiefly controls the production of specific proteins, which in turn affects the traits of the individual. Changes (mutations) to genes can result in changes to proteins, which can affect the structures and functions of the organism and thereby change traits (MS-LS3–1)

LS3.A: Inheritance of Traits – Variations of inherited traits between parent and offspring arise from genetic differences that result from the subset of chromosomes (and therefore genes) inherited (MS-LS3–2)

LS3.B: Variation of Traits – In sexually reproducing organisms, each parent contributes half of the genes ac-quired (at random) by the offspring. Individuals have two of each chromosome and hence two alleles of each gene, one acquired from each parent. These versions may be identical or may differ from each other (MS-LS3–2)

LS3.B: Variation of Traits – In addition to variations that arise from sexual reproduction, genetic information can be altered because of mutations. Though rare, mutations may result in changes to the structure and function of proteins. Some changes are beneficial, others harmful, and some neutral to the organism (MS-LS3–1)

Continued

NATIONAL SCIENCE TEACHING ASSOCIATION

Table 4.12. (*continued*)

Science and Engineering Practices

CONSTRUCTING EXPLANATIONS AND DESIGNING SOLUTIONS – Constructing explanations and designing solutions in 6–8 builds on K–5 experiences and progresses to include constructing explanations and designing solutions supported by multiple sources of evidence consistent with scientific ideas, principles, and theories. Apply scientific ideas to construct an explanation for realworld phenomena, examples, or events. (MS-LS4–2); Construct an explanation that includes qualitative or quantitative relationships between variables that describe phenomena (MS-LS4–4) OBTAINING, EVALUATING, AND COMMUNICATING INFORMATION – Obtaining, evaluating, and communicating information in 6–8 builds on K–5 experiences and progresses to evaluating the merit and validity of ideas and methods. Gather, read, and synthesize information from multiple appropriate sources and assess the credibility, accuracy, and possible bias of each publication and methods used, and describe how they are supported or not supported by evidence (MS-LS4–5)

Common Core Mathematics Standards

N/A

Common Core English Language Arts Standards

Writing Standards

W.7.1.A – Introduce claim(s), acknowledge alternate or opposing claims, and organize the reasons and evidence logically.

W.7.1.B – Support claim(s) with logical reasoning and relevant evidence, using accurate, credible sources and demonstrating an understanding of the topic or text.

W.7.1.C – Use words, phrases, and clauses to create cohesion and clarify the relationships among claim(s), reasons, and evidence.

W.7.1.E – Provide a concluding statement or section that follows from and supports the argument presented.

W.7.2.A – Introduce a topic clearly, previewing what is to follow; organize ideas, concepts, and information, using strategies such as definition, classification, comparison/contrast, and cause/effect; include formatting (e.g., headings), graphics (e.g., charts, tables), and multimedia when useful to aiding com-prehension.

W.7.2.B – Develop the topic with relevant facts, definitions, concrete details, quotations, or other information and examples.

W.7.3 – Write narratives to develop real or imagined experiences or events using effective technique, relevant descriptive details, and well-structured event sequences.W.7.6 – Use technology, including the Internet, to produce and publish writing and link to and cite sources as well as to interact and collaborate with others, including linking to and citing sources.

W.7.7 – Conduct short research projects to answer a question, drawing on several sources and generating additional related, focused questions for further research and investigation.

Reading Standards

RI.7.8 – Trace and evaluate the argument and specific claims in a text, assessing whether the reasoning is sound and the evidence is relevant and sufficient to support the claims.

RI.7.9 – Analyze how two or more authors writing about the same topic shape their presentations of key information by emphasizing different evidence or advancing different interpretations of facts.

21ST CENTURY SKILLS

Critical Thinking and Problem Solving, Communication and Collaboration, Information Literacy, Media Literacy

---

Table 4.13. Key Vocabulary for Lesson Four

Key Vocabulary	Definition
Mutation	Change in DNA sequence that may result in an altered or dysfunctional trait
Selective Breeding/Artificial Selection	Process by which humans select organisms with specific traits of interest to breed with one another in order to select for a particular trait in the offspring. This method has been used to domesticate plants and animals for human purposes.

TEACHER BACKGROUND INFORMATION

Science

For many centuries, humans have been modifying the genetic makeup of organisms to domesticate them for our own use. This has been done largely through the use of selective breeding (artificial selection) in which organisms with desired traits are allowed to reproduce with one another. Once scientists discovered that these traits were explained by the genetic makeup of the organisms and that mutations can alter the trait, attempts were made to speed up the process of modifying genes through irradiating seeds. This process proved to be too unreliable since the mutations were random and did not necessarily produce the desired traits. The growing understanding of genes and the development of various gene transfer technologies has allowed us to be more precise in moving genes of interest.

English Language Arts

Creating a documentary may be a new task for you and your students. There are numerous resources available to give you some guidance for how to approach this process. Below are examples of resources that may be helpful to you and your students:

- How to Create a Good Documentary – http://www.wikihow.com/Create-a-Good-Documentary-Film.

- Desktop Documentaries – http://www.desktop-documentaries.com/making-documentaries.html.

LESSON PREPARATION
English Language Arts

Each group of students should be assigned a different sections of the documentary. Each section will be limited to 10 min:

- Group 1

  o   What is a GMO? How are they created?
  o   What are examples of GMOs that currently exist?
  o   How have organisms' genetic makeups been altered in the past?

- Group 2

  o   What are possible benefits from GMOs in agriculture?

- Group 3

  o   What are possible threats from GMOs in agriculture?

- Group 4

  o   Who are the stakeholders and what are their stances?

- Group 5

  o   What is the government at the local, state, and federal levels doing to address the concerns of stakeholders?

Interviewing stakeholders would make student documentaries more authentic. However, most students will not know how to identify or contact individuals to interview. To assist them, prepare a list of people ahead of time who are willing to be interviewed and appear in the documentary. The types of individuals recruited will depend on the focus of the group. For instance, group 1 may want to interview their biology teacher or someone with expertise on the science of GMOs. Group 2 may want to interview stakeholders who support GMOs while Group 3 may want to interview stakeholders who oppose GMOs. These groups should focus the interview on the perceived benefits or threats of GMOs,. Group 4 might also want to interview stakeholders about their perspectives and why GMOs are an important issue to them. Students in group 4 could collaborate with groups 2 and 3 to combine their interview questions so that individuals are only interviewed once. Group 5 might want to interview their social studies teacher or individuals from the state or federal government that are directly involved. All groups may wish to use clips of interviews from other sources (like news clips). Be sure that students understand that they will need to get permission from the source before they can use a clip. As an alternative, students can summarize the information from the clip and provide quotes without actually showing the video clip.

Safety Considerations

- Students will be accessing information using the internet. Care should be taken to protect students from accessing internet sites that are inappropriate. Your IT contact person can provide guidance for appropriate search engines. Additionally, they may already have protective measures in place to prevent the students from accessing inappropriate content.

- Students will be interviewing adults outside of the school. Working with adults not affiliated with the school should require parental or teacher supervision.

SAMPLE MISCONCEPTIONS IN THIS LESSON
Science

- Students may think that mutation occurs because the organisms needs a particular trait to be successful in the environment.

SAMPLE DIFFERENTIATION STRATEGIES FOR THIS LESSON
Science

- Content – More advanced can be asked to think more deeply about the activities occurring during development at the cellular level. Khan Academy offers a basic introduction to genetic engineering at this site – https://www.khanacademy.org/science/high-school-biology/hs-molecular-genetics/hs-biotechnology/v/introduction-to-genetic-engineering

- Process – All students will be evaluated on their conceptual understanding in their notebook.

However, notebooks could be completed in digital format that allows for images and audio recording. Products could be differentiated along a range of recording basic knowledge of seeds and their function to a complex argument demonstrating differences across species.

- Product – All students will be evaluated on their conceptual understanding in their notebook. However, notebooks could be completed in digital format that allows for images and audio recording, rather than focusing on only written evidence of learning.

Mathematics

N/A

English Language Arts

- Process – Provide fewer, selected resources initially for students to examine and consider relevance, reliability, and relevance in order to support students. Focus on each of the concepts separately and then return to the same resources to discuss the next concept will also provide more support. Finally, allowing for multiple opportunities to get feedback on the resource selection assignment would support those students who are progressing more slowly.

- Product – Students can use multiple methods to complete the appropriate resource selection assignment. Additionally, a range of resources can be required depending on the students.

Social studies

- Content – Depending on their level, students could be asked to focus on a specific question, a group of questions or all of the of primary questions identified on Day 1. Different questions may be more or less difficult to answer, depending on the students ability to use the internet, ability to use good search terms and self-regulation skills.

- Process – Support from the teacher in this activity can range depending on the needs of the students. At the minimum level of support, teachers can provide guiding instructions to more capable students. For students who need more support, teachers can provide scaffolding such as identifying a few search terms and pointing out what makes a resource reliable. For students who need extra guidance, the teacher can model the process of research by finding a few resources then coaching students on how to use those resources to find terms to search for new resources.

- Product – Students can use multiple methods to complete the appropriate resource selection assignment. Additionally, fewer or more resources can be required depending on the students.

LEARNING PLAN COMPONENTS
INTRODUCTORY ACTIVITY/ENGAGEMENT
Science connections: DNA and Its Role

Day 16: Students share their ideas from their homework assignment (see Day 15 in Lesson 3) in which they made recommendations to farmers based on their knowledge. Help the students focus on the fact that they are suggesting that farmers manipulate the environment because they found that the environment influences the plants.

So far, students have seen that changing the environmental conditions, for example adding fertilizer, can alter plant form. This helps students understand that the environment influences organisms' growth and development. In order to help them recognize that there is variability in the plants as a result of variability in genes is a bit more challenging. Ask students to consider what they would expect in terms of variation in plant growth and development when the plants are all grown under the same conditions. Use data from the plants grown under the same conditions to show that even these plants had variation in some of the variables as well. Ask students to consider where this variation came from. Ask students to recall what they know about DNA and its function (this is pre-requisite knowledge for this module) and guide them to a recognition that these differences are likely a result of differences in DNA.

Mathematics connections

N/A

English Language Arts connections – Documentary Development

Day 16: Start by showing the following segment from the Jimmy Kimmel show: https://www.youtube.com/watch?v=EzEr23XJwFY. Discuss with the students that they will be creating a documentary as a class. They will start work on their documentary by creating a 5-minute video introducing the GMOs and the issues surrounding their use. They should interview faculty and students about what they know about GMOs, using these interviews to focus on the lack of complete understanding of the issue and highlighting the opposing viewpoints concerning GMOs. The teacher will be responsible for organizing and editing the introduction as a model for how the students will complete their segments of the documentary. Each group of students should be assigned a different sections of the documentary. Each section will be limited to 10 min:

- Group 1
    o What is a GMO? How are they created?
    o What are examples of GMOs that currently exist?
    o How have organisms' genetic makeups been altered in the past?
- Group 2
    o What are possible benefits from GMOs in agriculture?
- Group 3
    o What are possible threats from GMOs in agriculture?
- Group 4
    o Who are the stakeholders and what are their stances?
- Group 5
    o What is the government at the local, state, and federal levels doing to address the concerns of stakeholders?

In order to plan for the documentary, use the following steps:

1. Organize the structure and information that will be in the documentary. Based on what students know about GMOs, they should be able to decide what information is most important to share regarding their focus. They should consider that they will need to have a way to get the viewers interested in their topic, to figure out what is most important information to convey to inform their viewers, and a way to end the video that ties it all together.

2. Identify individuals who are willing to be interviewed and who will add credibility to their documentary. Generate interview questions based on the group focus and video interviews

3. Create storyboard and script

4. Shoot and edit the video

Social Studies class – What Role Does the Media Play in Policy Development?

Day 16: Discuss with students how they have obtained information about GMOs. Most of the information they are using was found on the Internet. Have students discuss how they would go about getting information without the Internet. Have students individually create a flowchart of their processes for finding relevant resources in their STEM Research Notebook. When they are finished, they should pair up and share their flowchart with their partner. Next, hold a whole class discussion of the process, creating a flowchart that represents student's general processes for finding relevant information on the board.

ACTIVITY/INVESTIGATION
Science connections: DNA and Its Role

Days 16–17: Have the students observe examples of the different types of plants provided in the kit in Lesson 1. Have students respond to the following in their STEM research notebooks (under the heading Differences in Fast-Plants):

- Describe how each plant appears to be unique compared to the others.

- Using what you know about plant structure and function, describe how you think this difference might make the plant better or worse at functioning?

After discussing the two questions above, lead a discussion to encourage students to recognize that differences in DNA can play an important role in helping some plants function better than others. Ask why the plants' DNA might vary. Focus students on the idea of mutations changing the plants' DNA. One way that mutation can happen is through

radiation. If you are using the Wisconsin Fast-Plants ™kit, point out that some plants that have been irradiated at different levels. We expect to see more mutations in the DNA of plants exposed to greater irradiation, resulting in increased differences in traits.

Remind students that they planted three groups of Fast-Plants ™ several weeks back representing three different experiments. The first experiment focused on the influence of fertilizer levels on plant growth and development. A second group of seeds they planted were all irradiated for different lengths of time. The assumption is that the more radiation the plants are exposed to, the more mutations would occur. They have already summarized the measurements for those plants in mathematics. Now they are going to examine the data in light of the research question – do changes in radiation levels influence the growth and development of the plants?

Students should start a new heading in their STEM research notebook entitled: Effects of Radiation of Wisconsin Fast-Plants™. Under this heading they will summarize the data from the radiation experiments collected earlier. They should discuss any major trends they observe and reflect on whether these trends might help or hurt the plants' function. Students should conclude that mutations caused by radiation are random and that with more mutations occurring the plants are likely to have more problems functioning. Discuss these findings with students.

Day 18: Ask students, "If we want to use our understanding of plants and genetics to get plants that are better suited for our agricultural needs, how can we do that?" Students should understand, as a result of the conversations they have had in social studies, that genetically modifying organisms is possible. Have students re-watch the Kickstarter video https://www.youtube.com/watch?v=YxFQ9MkwbDs. Remind them that they watched this video in social studies class to introduce them to the potential benefits of GMOs. Highlight that this company has since suspended the project of creating glowing plants (more information can be found at https://www.wired.com/story/inside-the-glowing-plant-startup-that-just-gave-up-its-quest/). One of the reasons that they suspended the project was because they found it challenging to get the plants to glow intensely enough to replace the street lamps. But the summary process they described is largely how many genetically engineered plants are created today.

Tell students that they are going to figure out the ways in which we have genetically modified plants. Instruct students to add a new heading in their STEM research notebook titled– Methods of Genetically Modifying Organisms. Students will complete a webquest, working in groups, and should identify three methods of genetic modification and answer the following questions in their STEM research notebook:

- What are methods used to genetically modify organisms currently used in agriculture?

- What are examples of specific plants and traits that these methods have been used with?

Student groups should share their three examples with the class. Compile a class list of all the unique examples on the board. Students should add these methods to their STEM research notebooks.

Mathematics connections

N/A

English Language Arts connections – Documentary Development

Day 16: Now that student groups have their assignments for the documentary, they should begin organizing the information necessary for their portion of the video. They will need to provide a list of information they think is most reasonable and would fit within the timeframe (under 10 minutes). They should provide some ideas for how they could get the viewers interested in their topic and how they will end the video in a way that ties it all together.

Day 17: Students will present their ideas to the class, focusing on the important ideas first, and then sharing the opening and closing ideas. Their peers will provide feedback regarding all of the components.

Day 18: Students will identify potential people to interview and work with you to design a set of interview questions to ask. Teach students how to use the video cameras for conducting the interviews.

Days 19–20: Conduct interviews.

Social Studies class – What Role Does the Media Play in Policy Development?

Day 16: Have students interview adults in the school (teachers, librarians, secretaries, principals) and family members to learn about how they accessed information before the advent of the Internet.

Days 17–18: Students will share how the adults they interviewed accessed information in the pre-Internet era. Students should find that books, magazines, newspapers, news radio, word of mouth were often used. Spend the rest of the class looking at newspaper articles and compare the information in these articles it with information from websites they used in their previous review of resources. Students should be able to conclude that reputable newspapers will often provide balanced reporting showing both sides of an issue whereas websites may report unbalanced or biased information in attempts to convince the reader to adopt a particular viewpoint rather than to simply inform. Emphasize to students, however, that reports in newspapers can also be biased depending upon factors such as the newspaper's ownership and readership.

EXPLAIN

Science connections: DNA and Its Role

Days 19–20: Discuss with students that humans were farming long before the technology for genetic modification came along. We have, however, been able to make changes to plants for millennia. Ask students how this is possible. Tell students that the methods farmers have been using for ages are the same ones used to generate the differences in the Fast Plants they looked at earlier in the week. Have students create a new heading in their STEM research notebooks entitled: Modifying Plant Genes the Old Fashion Way.

Have students go to the Fast Plants website (fastplants.org) to learn about how these plants were developed (http://www.fastplants.org/about/history.php). Have students describe in their notebooks the method used by Dr. Williams to generate the plants.

Then, have students go to the website http://www.vegetablefacts.net/ and identify one vegetable and describe its history using this and other websites, focusing on:

- Where did it originate?

- Why did humans domesticate it?

- How is the modern vegetable different from the ancestor?

- What varieties of the vegetable are now available on the market and how do they differ?

Have students identify one fruit they like and use the Internet to find the answers to the following questions:

- Where did it originate?

- Why did humans domesticate it?

- How is the modern fruit different from the ancestor?

- What varieties of the fruit are now available on the market and how do they differ?

Mathematics connections

N/A

English Language Arts connections

N/A

Social Studies class – What Role Does the Media Play in Policy Development?

Day 18: Students will discuss their findings about information access in the pre-Internet era then talk about the implications of the proliferation of information on the Internet for building an informed citizenry currently and in the future.

Read the *EcoWatch* article regarding Bill Nye's change in position about GMO's found at http://ecowatch.com/2015/07/14/was-bill-nye-paid-by-monsanto-gmos/. Next, have students examine the comments provided by readers, highlighting the fact that the Internet has provided more opportunities for citizens to participate in conversations about these types of issues.

Watch videos from different groups that show specific stances and some that may broadcast incorrect information, highlighting the fact that the Internet allows more opportunity for polarizing the debate as well as allowing more inaccurate information to be propagated.

Students can watch videos such as those below to determine if these provide balanced or biased information:

- https://www.youtube.com/watch?v=KGqQV6ObFCQ

- https://www.youtube.com/watch?v=M_ztZGbLEJ0

- https://www.youtube.com/watch?v=sH4bi60alZU

- https://www.youtube.com/watch?v=mSDldolwfvo

- https://www.youtube.com/watch?v=3eZDxtIhXZQ

- https://www.youtube.com/watch?v=8z_CqyB1dQo

Hold a class discussion asking students what we, as citizens, should do to become well informed? Encourage students to be cautious about using Internet sources and emphasize that they should cross-check information and look for balanced reporting.

EXTEND/APPLY KNOWLEDGE
Science connections: DNA and Its Role

Day 20: Students should share their findings from their exploration of the ways we have modified plants through selective breeding.

Mathematics connections

N/A

English Language Arts connections

N/A

Social Studies class – What Role Does the Media Play in Policy Development?

Day 19: Remind students that they have been exploring methods other than modern gene transfer technologies that humans have used to genetically modify organisms. In particular, remind students how humans have domesticated and modified organisms for use in agriculture using selective breeding. This practice has been

used for centuries and yet there isn't the same backlash against these methods that there is against GMO technology. Ask students why they think there is such a different response to such a similar activity. In particular, does the acceptance of a long-standing practice such as selective breeding suggest that we will eventually accept GMOs? As students to consider how they could communicate this dichotomy within the documentary.

EVALUATE/ASSESSMENT

Performance Tasks (see rubric attached):

1. Class participation rubric – Students will participate in whole class discussions, making claims that are backed up by evidence and reasoning.

2. Structure and content of documentary presentations – students will provide a list of the most important information they think should be conveyed in their portion of the documentary as well the way they will start and end the section.

3. STEM research notebook – students will be keeping a research notebook with both entries regarding their experiment as well as answer to questions from webquests.

Other Measures

2. STEM research notebook entries- reviewed by the science teacher

4

INTERNET RESOURCES
Science

- https://www.youtube.com/watch?v=YxFQ9MkwbDs

- http://www.fastplants.org/about/history.php

- http://www.vegetablefacts.net/

- https://www.khanacademy.org/science/high-school-biology/hs-molecular-genetics/hs-biotechnology/v/introduction-to-genetic-engineering

Mathematics

N/A

English Language Arts

- http://www.wikihow.com/Create-a-Good-Documentary-Film

- http://www.desktop-documentaries.com/making-documentaries.html

Social Studies

- http://ecowatch.com/2015/07/14/was-bill-nye-paid-by-monsanto-gmos/

- https://www.youtube.com/watch?v=KGqQV6ObFCQ

- https://www.youtube.com/watch?v=M_ztZGbLEJ0

- https://www.youtube.com/watch?v=sH4bi60alZU

- https://www.youtube.com/watch?v=mSDldolwfvo

- https://www.youtube.com/watch?v=3eZDxtIhXZQ

- https://www.youtube.com/watch?v=8z_CqyB1dQo

Class Participation

Students will participate in whole class discussions, making claims that are backed up by evidence and reasoning. A rubric for participation in the whole class discussion is found below:

Characteristic	Emerging (1)	Proficient (2)	Exemplary (3)
Follows guidelines of intellectual discussion and is civil	Criticizes other people personally instead of being critical of ideas; doesn't use appropriate language	Challenges the idea but without reason; uses appropriate language	Challenges the idea with solid reasoning; uses appropriate language; diverts any unproductive discussion
Makes claim	Claim unoriginal AND indirectly related to topic	Claim original AND indirectly related to topic	Claim original AND directly related to topic
Uses reliable sources for evidence	Uses unreliable resources (such as Wikipedia or blog)	Only uses textbook as resource	Uses outside reliable resources (such as a scientific journal or .gov or .edu website)
Appropriate level of evidence	Opinion-based evidence	One piece of researched evidence	More than one piece of researched evidence
Responds to the content of the discussion	No response or unrelated to claim	Response is indirectly associated with claim	Response is aligned with claim
Connects with what prior person says	Unrelated to current discussion	Stay on topic, but makes no connection with person before them	Acknowledges prior person's idea and elaborates on what previous person says
Able to defend their claim/ rebuttal	Has no response	Has a response but cannot back up response	Has a response and is able to back up response with further evidence
Uses appropriate reasoning	Reasoning is disconnected from claim	Reasoning is superficially connected to claim	Reasoning directly connects claim to evidence

STEM Research Notebook Rubric

	Beginning	Progressing	Advanced
Entries related to experimental design			
Methods	Methods incomplete	Description of methods for planting seeds is clearly indicated BUT How each set of seeds were treated differently is not clear	Description of methods for planting seeds is clearly indicated AND How each set of seeds were treated differently within a particular experiment is clearly indicated
Raw Data	Daily data absent	Daily data present, but not easily found	Daily data are clearly indicated
Summarized Data	Data not organized in tables	Data organized in tables but no labels to indicate	Data organized in tables with clear labels for each column and row
Entries Related to Webquests			
Vocabulary	No vocabulary is used OR Vocabulary is not defined	Writing uses some vocabulary to convey the ideas OR Vocabulary isn't always defined	Writing effectively uses appropriate vocabulary to convey the ideas AND Vocabulary is defined
Use of facts and details	Few facts and details are provided	Facts and details chosen are not always appropriate for communicating ideas	Facts and details chosen are appropriate and effectively communicating the ideas
Use of examples	No examples are provided OR Examples do not communicate the ideas	Examples are provided to support ideas BUT Examples provided are too few OR Examples provided do not always effectively communicate the ideas	Examples are provided to support ideas AND All examples provided effectively communicate the ideas
Syntax	Uses poor sentence structure	Student mostly uses appropriate sentence structure	Student uses appropriate sentence structure
Overall Organization	Organization is lacking	Organization is apparent, but is not effective in building understanding of the topic	Organization effectively builds understanding of the topic
Answers Questions	Fewer than 3 questions are answered thoroughly	3 of the 4 questions are answered thoroughly	All questions are answered thoroughly

Lesson Plan 5: Putting It All Together

LESSON SUMMARY

Students will spend this lesson organizing and producing their 10-minute documentary segments. English Language Arts is the lead for this lesson, however class time in other subject areas can be used to examine the accuracy of information and provide more time to develop the documentary. Students may need a most of the first three days to complete the entire documentary and have it ready for initial review on the fourth day and then for sharing with parents and friends on the fifth day.

ESSENTIAL QUESTION(S)

- How do we organize our information and interviews to make a coherent documentary?

ESTABLISHED GOALS/OBJECTIVES

- Students will be able to use storyboarding to organize their documentary for both shooting video, writing script, and editing.

- Students will demonstrate their scientific understanding of GMOs and the societal issues surrounding the use of GMOs by creating a documentary.

- Students will demonstrate their ability to collaborate with peers to organize information and create a product.

TIME REQUIRED – 5 DAYS (45-MINUTE CLASS PERIODS)

NECESSARY MATERIALS

- Video cameras and tripods
- Computers with video editing software and Internet access

Table 4.14. Standards Addressed in STEM Road Map Module Lesson

---

NEXT GENERATION SCIENCE STANDARDS

PERFORMANCE OBJECTIVES
N/A

Disciplinary Core Ideas and Crosscutting Concepts
N/A

Science and Engineering Practices
OBTAINING, EVALUATING, AND COMMUNICATING INFORMATION – Obtaining, evaluating, and communicating information in 6–8 builds on K–5 experiences and progresses to evaluating the merit and validity of ideas and methods. Gather, read, and synthesize information from multiple appropriate sources and assess the credibility, accuracy, and possible bias of each publication and methods used, and describe how they are supported or not supported by evidence. (MS-LS4–5)

Common Core Mathematics Standards
N/A

COMMON CORE ENGLISH LANGUAGE ARTS STANDARDS

WRITING STANDARDS
W.7.1.A – Introduce claim(s), acknowledge alternate or opposing claims, and organize the reasons and evidence logically.
W.7.1.B – Support claim(s) with logical reasoning and relevant evidence, using accurate, credible sources and demonstrating an understanding of the topic or text.
W.7.1.C – Use words, phrases, and clauses to create cohesion and clarify the relationships among claim(s), reasons, and evidence.
W.7.1.E – Provide a concluding statement or section that follows from and supports the argument presented.
W.7.2.A – Introduce a topic clearly, previewing what is to follow; organize ideas, concepts, and information, using strategies such as definition, classification, comparison/contrast, and cause/effect; include formatting (e.g., headings), graphics (e.g., charts, tables), and multimedia when useful to aiding com-prehension.
W.7.2.B – Develop the topic with relevant facts, definitions, concrete details, quotations, or other information and examples.
W.7.3 – Write narratives to develop real or imagined experiences or events using effective technique, relevant descriptive details, and well-structured event sequences.
W.7.6 – Use technology, including the Internet, to produce and publish writing and link to and cite sources as well as to interact and collaborate with others, including linking to and citing sources.
W.7.7 – Conduct short research projects to answer a question, drawing on several sources and generating additional related, focused questions for further research and investigation.

READING STANDARDS
RI.7.8 – Trace and evaluate the argument and specific claims in a text, assessing whether the reasoning is sound and the evidence is relevant and sufficient to support the claims.RI.7.9 – Analyze how two or more authors writing about the same topic shape their presentations of key information by emphasizing different evidence or advancing different interpretations of facts.

21ST CENTURY SKILLS
Critical Thinking and Problem Solving; Communication and Collaboration; Information Literacy; Media Literacy

---

Table 4.15. Key Vocabulary for Lesson 5

Key Vocabulary	Definition
Storyboard	A way of visually organizing the flow of a video by using a sequence of drawings.

TEACHER BACKGROUND INFORMATION

Creating a documentary may be a new task for you and your students. There are numerous resources available to give you some guidance for how to approach this process. Below are examples of resources that may be helpful to you and your students:

- How to Create a Good Documentary – http://www.wikihow.com/Create-a-Good-Documentary-Film.

- Desktop Documentaries – http://www.desktop-documentaries.com/making-documentaries.html.

Most presentation software currently on the market offer an opportunity to create video from a set of slides that will include voice. This can be incorporated into the video as a way to share information and incorporate images beyond people talking to the camera.

LESSON PREPARATION

Students will be intensively working on their documentary during this lesson. It would be useful to have at least one Information Technology person from your school provide some guidance to students about using cameras and the video-editing software. Having additional staff on hand will allow groups to get just-in-time assistance tailored to their needs.

The videos will be presented to other parents, friends, and family, in the students' classrooms during a video Premier night. Afterward, the students will lead a discussion with their family and friends to determine what perspectives these individuals have about the GMO issue after viewing the video. Have the classrooms reserved and the appropriate projection equipment in each classroom. Provide some guiding questions to the student-led groups such as:

- What did you know about GMO's before the documentary? What did you learn new?

- Where do you identify yourself as a stakeholder?

- Do you think we should continue to pursue GMO research? Why?

- What is your stance on labeling goods that contain GMO's as having GMO's? Why?

Safety Considerations

- Students will be accessing information using the internet. Care should be taken to protect students from accessing internet sites that are inappropriate. Your IT contact person can provide guidance for appropriate search engines. Additionally, they may already have protective measures in place to prevent the students from accessing inappropriate content.

LEARNING PLAN COMPONENTS
INTRODUCTORY ACTIVITY/ENGAGEMENT

Science connections

N/A

Mathematics connections

N/A

English Language Arts connections – Documentary Development

Day 21: Students should have their interviews complete and information gathered. Ask them to consider how they might organize their ideas into their documentary. Encourage students to think about what video shots they would want to address the ideas they want to incorporate into their segment. Introduce the idea of storyboarding being a visual way to organize their documentary segments, showing each planned video shot and the flow of ideas in each.

Social Studies class

N/A

ACTIVITY/INVESTIGATION

Science connections – Documentary Development

Days 21–24: Students should work on their documentary shooting or editing as well as get feedback from peers and from you regarding the accuracy of information and their storyboard ideas.

Mathematics connections

N/A

English Language Arts connections – Documentary Development

Days 21–24: Students storyboard their documentary using presentation software. They should also identify scenes that still need to be recorded.

Social Studies class – Documentary Development

Days 22–24: Students should work on their documentary shooting or editing video as well as get feedback from peers and from you regarding the accuracy of information and their storyboard ideas.

EXPLAIN

Science connections

N/A

Mathematics connections

N/A

English Language Arts connections – Documentary Development

Days 22–23: Students should be provided instruction on how to get started using the presentation software for video recording as well as how to use the editing software.

Social Studies class

N/A

EXTEND/APPLY KNOWLEDGE

Science connections

N/A

Mathematics connections

N/A

English Language Arts connections

N/A

Social Studies class – Documentary Development

Day 25: Students should complete their editing and will share their final video with the class. The class will discuss the experience of creating the documentary.

Day 25: The videos will be presented to other parents, friends, and family, in the students' classrooms during the video Premier night. Afterward, the students will lead a discussion with their family and friends to determine what perspectives these individuals have about the GMO issue after viewing the video.

EVALUATE/ASSESSMENT

Performance Tasks (see rubrics attached):

1. Collaboration

2. Complete Documentary

Other Measures
N/A

INTERNET RESOURCES
Science

N/A

Mathematics

N/A

English Language Arts

- http://www.wikihow.com/Create-a-Good-Documentary-Film

- http://www.desktop-documentaries.com/making-documentaries.html

Social Studies

N/A

Rubric for Collaboration

	Beginning	Progressing	Advanced
Participation	Disengaged, does not provide helpful contributions	Provides some helpful contributions	Fully engages with the project by consistently making helpful contributions
On task	Rarely on task	Sometimes is on task but loses focus	Works with the group to try to stay focused on the task at hand
Cooperation with others – working	Rarely works on tasks with others OR Rarely completes tasks assigned by the group	Sometimes works on tasks with others OR Sometimes completes tasks assigned by the group	Consistently works on tasks with others AND Always completes tasks assigned by the group
Cooperation with others – communication	DOES LESS THAN TWO OF THE FOLLOWING: • Respectful of differing opinion in all communications with team mates • Listens to what others in the group are saying and responds appropriately • Communications to the group provide effective feedback	DOES ANY TWO OF THE FOLLOWING: • Respectful of differing opinion in all communications with team mates • Listens to what others in the group are saying and responds appropriately • Communications to the group provide effective feedback	DOES ALL OF THE FOLLOWING: • Respectful of differing opinion in all communications with team mates • Listens to what others in the group are saying and responds appropriately • Communications to the group provide effective feedback

Rubric for the documentary

	Beginning	Progressing	Advanced
Vocabulary	No vocabulary is used OR Vocabulary is never defined	Uses some vocabulary to convey the ideas OR Vocabulary isn't always defined	Effectively uses important vocabulary to convey the ideas AND Vocabulary is defined
Use of facts and details	Few facts and details are provided	Facts and details chosen are not always appropriate for communicating the idea	Facts and details chosen are appropriate, effectively communicating the idea
Use of examples	No examples are provided OR Examples do not communicate the ideas	Examples are provided to support ideas BUT Examples provided are too few OR Examples provided do not always effectively communicate the ideas	Examples are provided to support ideas AND All examples provided effectively communicate the ideas
Overall Organization	Organization is lacking	Organization is apparent, but is not effective building understanding in the viewer	Organization effectively builds understanding in the viewer

REFERENCES

Johnson, C. C., Moore, T. J., Utley, J., Breiner, J., Burton, S. R., Peter-Burton, E. E., Walton, J., and Parton, C. L. 2015. The STEM road map for grades 6-8. In C. C. Johnson, E. E. Peters-Burton, and T. J. Moore (Eds.), *STEM road map: A framework for integrated STEM education* (pp. 96–123). New York, NY: Routledge.

WIDA Consortium. 2012. 2012 Amplification of the English language development standards: Kindergarten-grade 12. Retrieved from https://www.wida.us/standards/eld.aspx

5

TRANSFORMING LEARNING WITH GENETICALLY MODIFIED ORGANISMS AND THE *STEM ROAD MAP CURRICULUM SERIES*

Carla C. Johnson

This chapter serves as a conclusion to the Genetically Modified Organisms integrated STEM curriculum module, but it is just the beginning of the transformation of your classroom that is possible through use of the *STEM Road Map Curriculum Series*. In this book, many key resources have been provided to make learning meaningful for your students through integration of science, technology, engineering, and mathematics, as well as social studies and English language arts, into powerful problem- and project-based instruction. First, the Genetically Modified Organisms curriculum is grounded in the latest theory of learning for students in Grade 7 specifically. Second, as your students work through this module, they engage in using the engineering design process (EDP) and build prototypes like engineers and STEM professionals in the real world. Third, students acquire important knowledge and skills grounded in national academic standards in mathematics, English language arts, science, and 21st century skills that will enable their learning to be deeper, retained longer, and applied throughout, illustrating the critical connections within and across disciplines. Finally, authentic formative assessments, including strategies for differentiation and addressing misconceptions, are embedded within the curriculum activities.

The Genetically Modified Organisms curriculum in the Optimizing the Human Condition STEM Road Map theme can be used in single-content classrooms (e.g., mathematics) where there is only one teacher or expanded to include multiple teachers and content areas across classrooms. Through the exploration of the GMO Documentary, students engage in a real-world STEM problem on the first day of

DOI: 10.4324/9781003261735-7

instruction and gather necessary knowledge and skills along the way in the context of solving the problem.

The other topics in the *STEM Road Map Curriculum Series* are designed in a similar manner, and NSTA Press and Routledge have published additional volumes in this series for this and other grade levels, and have plans to publish more.

For an up-to-date list of volumes in the series, please visit https://www.routledge.com/STEM-Road-Map-Curriculum-Series/book-series/SRM (for titles co-published by Routledge and NSTA Press), or https://www.nsta.org/book-series/stem-road-map-curriculum (for titles published by NSTA Press).

If you are interested in professional development opportunities focused on the STEM Road Map specifically or integrated STEM or STEM programs and schools overall, contact the lead editor of this project, Dr. Carla C. Johnson, Professor of Science Education at NC State University (carlacjohnson@ncsu.edu). Someone from the team will be in touch to design a program that will meet your individual, school, or district needs.

APPENDIX

CONTENT STANDARDS ADDRESSED
IN THIS MODULE

Table A.1. Next Generation Science Standards (NGSS)

Performance Expectations	Disciplinary Core Ideas and Crosscutting Concepts	Science and Engineering Practices
MS-LS1-3 – Use argument supported by evidence for how the body is a system of interacting subsystems composed of groups of cells. MS-LS1-5 – Construct a scientific explanation based on evidence for how environmental and genetic factors influence the growth of organisms. MS-LS4-5 – Gather and synthesize information about the technologies that have changed the way humans influence the inheritance of desired traits in organisms.	**Disciplinary Core Ideas** • LS1.A: Structure and Function – In multicellular organisms, the body is a system of multiple interacting subsystems. These subsystems are groups of cells that work together to form tissues and organs that are specialized for particular body functions (MS-LS1-3) • LS1.B: Growth and Development of Organisms – Organisms reproduce, either sexually or asexually, and transfer their genetic information to their offspring (secondary to MSLS3-2) • LS3.A: Inheritance of Traits – Genes are located in the chromosomes of cells, with each chromosome pair containing two variants of each of many distinct genes. Each distinct gene chiefly controls the production of specific proteins, which in turn affects the traits of the individual. Changes (mutations) to genes can result in changes to proteins, which can affect the structures and functions of the organism and thereby change traits (MS-LS3-1). • LS3.A: Inheritance of Traits – Variations of inherited traits between parent and offspring arise from genetic differences that result from the subset of chromosomes (and therefore genes) inherited (MS-LS3-2) • LS3.B: Variation of Traits – In sexually reproducing organisms, each parent contributes half of the genes acquired (at random) by the offspring. Individuals have two of each chromosome and hence two alleles of each gene, one acquired from each parent. These versions may be identical or may differ from each other (MS-LS3-2) • LS3.B: Variation of Traits – In addition to variations that arise from sexual reproduction, genetic information can be altered because of mutations. Though rare, mutations may result in changes to the structure and function of proteins. Some changes are beneficial, others harmful, and some neutral to the organism (MS-LS3-1)	*Developing and Using Models* • Develop and use a model to describe phenomena (MS-LS3-1),(MS-LS3-2) *Analyzing and Interpreting Data* • Analyze displays of data to identify linear and nonlinear relationships (MS-LS4-3) • Analyze and interpret data to determine similarities and differences in findings (MS-LS4-1) *Using Mathematics and Computational Thinking* • Use mathematical representations to support scientific conclusions and design solutions (MS-LS4-6) *Constructing Explanations and Designing Solutions* • Apply scientific ideas to construct an explanation for realworld phenomena, examples, or events (MS-LS4-2) • Construct an explanation that includes qualitative or quantitative relationships between variables that describe phenomena (MS-LS4-4) *Obtaining, Evaluating, and Communicating Information* • Gather, read, and synthesize information from multiple appropriate sources and assess the credibility, accuracy, and possible bias of each publication and methods used, and describe how they are supported or not supported by evidence (MS-LS4-5)

Table A.1. (*continued*)

Performance Expectations	Disciplinary Core Ideas and Crosscutting Concepts	Science and Engineering Practices
	Cross-Cutting Concepts *Patterns* • Macroscopic patterns are related to the nature of microscopic and atomic-level structure. • Graphs, charts, and images can be used to identify patterns in data. *Cause and Effect* • Phenomena may have more than one cause, and some cause and effect relationships in systems can only be described using probability. *Systems and Systems Models* • Systems may interact with other systems; they may have sub-systems and be a part of larger complex systems. • Models can be used to represent systems and their interactions – such as inputs, processes and outputs – and energy, matter, and information flows within systems. • Models are limited in that they only represent certain aspects of the system under study. *Structure and Function* • Complex and microscopic structures and systems can be visualized, modeled, and used to describe how their function depends on the shapes, composition, and relationships among its parts; therefore, complex natural and designed structures/systems can be analyzed to determine how they function. *Stability and Change* • Small changes in one part of a system might cause large changes in another part.	

Table A.2. Common Core Mathematics and English/Language Arts (English/Language Arts) Standards

Common Core Mathematics	Common Core English/Language Arts (English/Language Arts)
Mathematics Practices MP1 – Make sense of problems and persevere in solving them. MP3 – Construct viable arguments and critique the reasoning of others. **Mathematics Content** 7.RP.A.2 – Recognize and represent proportional relationships between quantities. 7.RP.A.2.C – Represent proportional relationships by equations. For ex-ample, if total cost t is proportional to the number n of items purchased at a constant price p, the relationship between the total cost and the number of items can be expressed as t = pn. 7.NS.A.1 – Apply and extend previous understandings of addition and subtraction to add and subtract rational numbers; represent addition and subtraction on a horizontal or vertical number line diagram. 7.NS.A.1.D – Apply properties of operations as strategies to add and sub-tract rational numbers. 7.NS.A.3 – Solve real-world and mathematical problems involving the four operations with rational numbers (Computations with rational numbers extend the rules for manipulating fractions to complex fractions).	**Writing Standards** W.7.1.A – Introduce claim(s), acknowledge alternate or opposing claims, and organize the reasons and evidence logically. W.7.1.B – Support claim(s) with logical reasoning and relevant evidence, using accurate, credible sources and demonstrating an understanding of the topic or text. W.7.1.C – Use words, phrases, and clauses to create cohesion and clarify the relationships among claim(s), reasons, and evidence. W.7.1.E – Provide a concluding statement or section that follows from and supports the argument presented. W.7.2.A – Introduce a topic clearly, previewing what is to follow; organize ideas, concepts, and information, using strategies such as definition, classification, comparison/contrast, and cause/effect; include formatting (e.g., headings), graphics (e.g., charts, tables), and multimedia when useful to aiding comprehension. W.7.2.B – Develop the topic with relevant facts, definitions, concrete details, quotations, or other information and examples. W.7.3 – Write narratives to develop real or imagined experiences or events using effective technique, relevant descriptive details, and well-structured event sequences. W.7.6 – Use technology, including the Internet, to produce and publish writing and link to and cite sources as well as to interact and collaborate with others, including linking to and citing sources. W.7.7 – Conduct short research projects to answer a question, drawing on several sources and generating additional related, focused questions for further research and investigation. **Reading Standards** RI.7.8 – Trace and evaluate the argument and specific claims in a text, assessing whether the reasoning is sound and the evidence is relevant and sufficient to support the claims. RI.7.9 – Analyze how two or more authors writing about the same topic shape their presentations of key information by emphasizing different evidence or advancing different interpretations of facts.

Table A.3. 21st Century Skills Addressed in STEM Road Map Module

21st Century Skills	Learning Skills and Technology Tools (from P21 framework)	Teaching Strategies	Evidence of Success
Interdisciplinary Themes	Environmental Literacy Financial, Economic, Business and Entrepreneurial literacy Civic Literacy	Teachers will lead a discussion of how GMO's can influence the environment Use cost-benefit analysis for evaluating economic viability of GMO in farming Discussion regarding the importance of being an informed citizen and how the local, state, and federal governments interact	Students will describe the concerns regarding the impact of GMO's in the environment in their communication and documentary Students will use cost-benefit analysis in their discussion of the GMO issue Students will discuss the importance of an informed citizenry and explain the current involvement of the government in their GMO documentary.
Learning and Innovation Skills	Critical Thinking and Problem Solving Communication and Collaboration	Students will investigate ways to effectively summarize information sources regarding the GMO issue Teacher will discuss ways to organize and communicate information	Students will generate rules to effectively summarize their sources they will use in their documentary Students will use storyboarding to organize their documentary
Information, Media and Technology Skills	Information Literacy	The students will investigate the use of the Internet to identify relevant and reliable sources	Students will create rules to identify reliable and relevant resources and use them in finding the sources for their documentary.
Life and Career Skills	Flexibility and Adaptability Initiative and Self-Direction Social and Cross Cultural Skills Productivity and Accountability Leadership and Responsibility	Teachers will create situations where students are able to work in groups collaboratively.	Students will work effectively in collaborative groups and be clear about roles of each member. Students will take responsibility for their own learning.

Table A.4. English Language Development Standards Addressed in STEM Road Map Module

English Language Development Standards: Grades 6–8 (WIDA, 2012)
ELD STANDARD 1: SOCIAL AND INSTRUCTIONAL LANGUAGE English language learners communicate for Social and Instructional purposes within the school setting.
ELD STANDARD 2: THE LANGUAGE OF LANGUAGE ARTS English language learners communicate information, ideas and concepts necessary for academic success in the content area of Language Arts.
ELD STANDARD 3: THE LANGUAGE OF MATHEMATICS English language learners communicate information, ideas and concepts necessary for academic success in the content area of Mathematics
ELD STANDARD 4: THE LANGUAGE OF SCIENCE. English language learners communicate information, ideas and concepts necessary for academic success in the content area of Science
ELD STANDARD 5: THE LANGUAGE OF SOCIAL STUDIES English language learners communicate information, ideas and concepts necessary for academic success in the content area of Social Studies.

INDEX

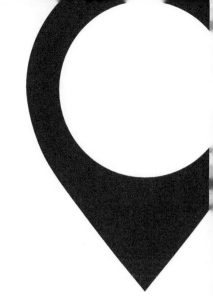

Note: Page numbers in **bold** type refer to tables
Page numbers in *italic* type refer to figures

NATIONAL SCIENCE TEACHING ASSOCIATION

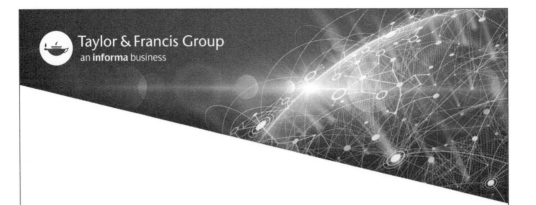

For Product Safety Concerns and Information please contact our
EU representative GPSR@taylorandfrancis.com Taylor & Francis
Verlag GmbH, Kaufingerstraße 24, 80331 München, Germany